Mike Holt's

JOURNEYMAN
SIMULATED EXAM

Theory • Code • Calculations

Suitable for all electrical exams based on the NEC®, such as:
AMP, ICC, Local/State Examining Boards, Pearson VUE, Prometric, Prov, PSI

Based on the 2014 NEC®

Mike Holt Enterprises, Inc.
888.NEC.CODE (632.2633) • www.MikeHolt.com

Date: May 13, 2014

NOTICE TO THE READER

Mike Holt's Journeyman Simulated Exam, based on the 2014 NEC®

First Printing: May 2014

Author: Mike Holt
Technical Illustrator: Mike Culbreath
Cover Design: Madalina Iordache-Levay
Layout Design and Typesetting: Cathleen Kwas

COPYRIGHT © 2014 Charles Michael Holt
ISBN 978-1-932685-62-6

Produced and Printed in the USA

This logo is a registered trademark of Mike Holt Enterprises, Inc.

If you are an instructor and would like to request an examination copy of this or other Mike Holt Publications:

Call: 888.NEC.CODE (632.2633) • Fax: 352.360.0983
E-mail: Info@MikeHolt.com • Visit: www.MikeHolt.com

You can download a sample PDF of all our publications by visiting www.MikeHolt.com

I dedicate this book to the
Lord Jesus Christ, my mentor and teacher

Mike Holt

Our Commitment

We are committed to serving the electrical industry with integrity and respect by always searching for the most accurate interpretation of the *NEC*® and creating the highest quality instructional material that makes learning easy.

We are invested in the idea of changing lives, and build our products with the goal of not only helping you meet your licensing requirements, but also with the goal that this knowledge will improve your expertise in the field and help you throughout your career.

We are committed to building a life-long relationship with you, and to helping you in each stage of your electrical career. Whether you are an apprentice just getting started in the industry, or an electrician preparing to take an exam, we are here to help you. When you need Continuing Education credits to renew your license, we will do everything we can to get our online courses and seminars approved in your state. Or if you are a contractor looking to train your team, we have a solution for you. And if you have advanced to the point where you are now teaching others, we are here to help you build your program and provide tools to make that task easier.

We genuinely care about providing quality electrical training that will help you take your skills to the next level.

Thanks for choosing Mike Holt Enterprises for your electrical training needs. We are here to help you every step of the way and encourage you to contact us so we can be a part of your success.

God bless,

TABLE OF CONTENTS

PART 1—ELECTRICAL THEORY

Part 2—*National Electrical Code®*

Part 3—Electrical Calculations

ABOUT THE AUTHOR

Mike Holt—Author

Founder and President
Mike Holt Enterprises
Groveland, FL
www.MikeHolt.com

Mike Holt worked his way up through the electrical trade. He began as an apprentice electrician and became one of the most recognized experts in the world as it relates to electrical power installations. He's worked as a journeyman electrician, master electrician, and electrical contractor. Mike's experience in the real world gives him a unique understanding of how the *NEC* relates to electrical installations from a practical standpoint. You'll find his writing style to be direct, nontechnical, and powerful.

Did you know Mike didn't finish high school? So if you struggled in high school or didn't finish at all, don't let it get you down. However, realizing that success depends on one's continuing pursuit of education, Mike immediately attained his GED, and ultimately attended the University of Miami's Graduate School for a Master's degree in Business Administration.

Mike resides in Central Florida, is the father of seven children, has five grandchildren, and enjoys many outside interests and activities. He's a nine-time National Barefoot Water-Ski Champion (1988, 1999, 2005–2009, 2012–2013). He's set many national records and continues to train year-round at a World competition level (www.barefootwaterskier.com).

What sets him apart from some is his commitment to living a balanced lifestyle; placing God first, family, career, then self.

Special Acknowledgments—First, I want to thank God for my godly wife who's always by my side and my children, Belynda, Melissa, Autumn, Steven, Michael, Meghan, and Brittney.

A special thank you must be sent to the staff at the National Fire Protection Association (NFPA), publishers of the *NEC*—in particular Jeff Sargent for his assistance in answering my many *Code* questions over the years. Jeff, you're a "first class" guy, and I admire your dedication and commitment to helping others understand the *NEC*. Other former NFPA staff members I would like to thank include John Caloggero, Joe Ross, and Dick Murray for their help in the past.

A personal thank you goes to Sarina, my long-time friend and office manager. It's been wonderful working side-by-side with you for over 25 years nurturing this company's growth from its small beginnings.

SIMULATED EXAM INSTRUCTIONS

General

This exam is intended to be used as a diagnostic tool to help you evaluate your preparation for taking an exam, and is not intended to be a duplication of any actual licensing exam. We suggest you use this exam to evaluate yourself to determine the areas in which you need to focus your studies to improve your test score. This exam is comprised of three parts:

Part 1—Electrical Theory (4-Hour Limit)
Part 2—*National Electrical Code* (4-Hour Limit)
Part 3—Electrical Calculations (5-Hour Limit)

Reference Books

Try to duplicate the exact conditions you will face on your exam. Use those reference books which you are permitted to bring into the testing room. You will find this list of reference materials in the Candidate Booklet provided by the state or the testing agency for your state. If your state does not allow the use of reference books other than the *NEC*, you should attempt this test using only the *NEC*.

Note: The time limits of the exam will prevent you from looking up all of the answers on the exam, so try to answer as many questions as possible without looking them up.

DO NOT LOOK AT ANY PART OF THE EXAM UNTIL THE APPROPRIATE TIME IN THE SCHEDULE.

Materials

You will need a blank sheet of paper, a calculator, approved reference books (see above), several pencils, and an alarm clock.

Grading Your Exam

Your score is important to you, but keep in mind that you are trying to determine your weakest areas so you know what you need to review. To grade your Answer Sheet, go to the Answer Keys beginning on page 35. Grade each Part separately. Use the following formula:

Score (Number Correct Answers) /Total Number of Questions x 100 = Percentage Correct

Part 1 Score _____ / 100 x 100 = _____%

Part 2 Score _____ / 100 x 100 = _____%

Part 3 Score _____ / 65 x 100 = _____%

Note: Any part of the exam on which you scored less than 75% is considered failing and additional study is needed. If, after taking these exams you determine that you need additional study, *Mike Holt's NEC Electrical Exam Preparation* textbook, *Basic Electrical Theory* textbook, and the *Understanding the National Electrical Code* textbooks with the related DVD training programs can help you with your studies.

Time Schedule

The total practice time for these Simulated Exams is 13 hours. We suggest that you do not take more than one Part a day. Use an alarm clock to mark your time so that you can stay focused and stay within the time allotted.

Adjust your starting and finish times to allow the same amount of testing time as given in the following examples:

Part 1—Electrical Theory

7:55 a.m.:	Have all your materials gathered and ready. Set the alarm for 12:00 noon., or set your timer for 4 hours (to mark the end of Part 1). Go to Page 51 and tear out the Part 1 Electrical Theory Answer Sheet to record your answers.
8:00 a.m.:	Go to Page 1 and begin Part 1—Electrical Theory Exam. Answer all questions as quickly and accurately as possible.
12:00 noon:	Part 1 is over, even if you are not finished.

Part 2—*National Electrical Code*

7:55 a.m.:	Set the alarm for 12:00 noon, or set your timer for 4 hours (to mark the end of Part 2). Go to Page 53 and tear out the Part 2 *National Electrical Code* Answer Sheet to record your answers. Use the *NEC* and any other permitted reference books.
8:00 a.m.:	Go to Page 13 and begin Part 2—*National Electrical Code.* Answer all questions as quickly and accurately as possible. Do NOT start Part 3
12:00 noon:	Part 2 is over, even if you are not finished.

Part 3—Electrical Calculations

7:55 a.m.:	Set the alarm for 1:00 p.m., or set your timer for 5 hours (to mark the end of Part 3). Go to Page 55 and tear out the Part 3 Electrical Calculations Answer Sheet to record your answers.
8:00 a.m.:	Go to Page 25 and begin Part 3—Electrical Calculations. Use blank paper to work out the calculations.
1:00 p.m.:	Part 3 is over, even if you are not finished.

PART 1

ELECTRICAL THEORY EXAM (4 HOURS)

The questions for this exam are extracted from *Mike Holt's Illustrated Guide to Basic Electrical Theory* textbook.

CHAPTER 1— ELECTRICAL FUNDAMENTALS

UNIT 1—MATTER

1. Providing a path to the earth often helps reduce electro-static charge.

    (a) True
    (b) False

2. Lightning frequently terminates to a point of elevation and strikes nonmetallic as well as metallic objects with the same frequency.

    (a) True
    (b) False

3. The termination of the lightning stroke is unlikely to ignite combustible materials.

    (a) True
    (b) False

4. Lightning protection is intended to protect the building itself, as well as the electrical equipment on or inside the structure.

    (a) True
    (b) False

UNIT 3—MAGNETISM

5. Nonmagnetic metals are ferrous, meaning they do not contain any iron, and cannot be magnetized.

    (a) True
    (b) False

6. Magnetic lines of force can cross each other and they are called flux lines.

    (a) True
    (b) False

UNIT 4—ELECTRICITY

7. It is not the force of the magnetic field through a conductor that produces electricity; it is the relative motion of the field to the electrons within the conductor that produces the movement of electrons.

    (a) True
    (b) False

8. People become injured and death occurs when voltage pushes electrons through the human body causing the heart to go into ventricular fibrillation.

    (a) True
    (b) False

9. The severity of an electric shock is dependent on the current flowing through the body, which is impacted by circuit voltage and contact resistance.

    (a) True
    (b) False

10. An electrical arc blast can approach _____, which vaporizes metal parts and produces an explosive and deadly pressure wave.

    (a) 10,000°F
    (b) 15,000°F
    (c) 25,000°F
    (d) 30,000°F

UNIT 5—ELECTROMAGNETISM

11. If a conductor carrying current is next to another conductor carrying current in the opposite direction, the electromagnetic field attempts to push the conductors apart.

    (a) True
    (b) False

UNIT 6—USES OF ELECTROMAGNETISM

12. A clamp-on ac ammeter has a coil that is clamped around the conductor and detects the rising and falling _____ field being produced due to the ac flow through the conductor.

    (a) static
    (b) current
    (c) power
    (d) magnetic

13. Ohmmeters measure the _____ or opposition to current flow of a circuit or component.

    (a) voltage
    (b) current
    (c) power
    (d) resistance

14. The megger is used to measure very high-_____ values, such as those found in cable insulation, or motor and transformer windings.

    (a) voltage
    (b) current
    (c) power
    (d) resistance

15. The electric motor works on the principle of the attracting and repelling forces of _____ fields.

    (a) voltage
    (b) current
    (c) power
    (d) magnetic

16. The _____ of a generator is forced to rotate while it is being subjected to the magnetic field of the stator.

    (a) winding
    (b) rotor
    (c) stator
    (d) b or c

17. A holding relay is primarily used for worker convenience.

    (a) True
    (b) False

CHAPTER 2—BASIC ELECTRICITY

UNIT 7—THE ELECTRICAL CIRCUIT

18. According to the Electron Current Flow Theory, electrons flow away from the negative terminal of the source, through the circuit and load, toward the positive terminal of the source.

    (a) True
    (b) False

19. According to the Conventional Current Flow Theory, electrons travel from positive to negative.

    (a) True
    (b) False

UNIT 9—ELECTRICAL FORMULAS

20. The major advantage of ac over dc is the ease of voltage regulation by the use of a transformer.

    (a) True
    (b) False

21. The best conductors, in order of their conductivity, are gold, silver, copper, and aluminum.

    (a) True
    (b) False

22. In a dc circuit, the only opposition to current flow is the physical resistance of the material. This opposition is called "reactance" and is measured in ohms.

    (a) True
    (b) False

23. What is the voltage drop of two 12 AWG conductors (0.40 ohms) supplying a 16A load, located 100 ft from the power supply? Formula: $E = I \times R$

    (a) 1.60V
    (b) 3.20V
    (c) 6.40V
    (d) 12.80V

24. What is the resistance of the circuit conductors when the conductor voltage drop is 7.20V and the current flow is 50A?

    (a) 0.14 ohms
    (b) 0.30 ohms
    (c) 3 ohms
    (d) 14 ohms

25. What is the power loss in watts of a conductor that carries 24A and has a voltage drop of 7.20V?

    (a) 175W
    (b) 350W
    (c) 700W
    (d) 2,400W

26. What is the approximate power consumed by a 10 kW heat strip rated 230V, when connected to a 208V circuit?

    (a) 8.2 kW
    (b) 9.5 kW
    (c) 11.3 kW
    (d) 12.4 kW

27. The formulas in the power wheel apply to _____.

    (a) dc
    (b) ac with unity power factor
    (c) dc or ac circuits
    (d) a and b

28. The total circuit resistance of two 12 AWG conductors (each 100 ft long) is 0.40 ohms. If the current of the circuit is 16A, what is the power loss of the conductors in watts?

    (a) 75W
    (b) 100W
    (c) 300W
    (d) 600W

29. What is the conductor power loss in watts for a 120V circuit that has a 3 percent voltage drop and carries a current flow of 12A?

    (a) 43W
    (b) 86W
    (c) 172W
    (d) 1,440W

30. What does it cost per year (at 8 cents per kWh) for the power loss of a 12 AWG circuit conductor (100 ft long) that has a total resistance of 0.40 ohm and current flow of 16A?

    (a) $30
    (b) $50
    (c) $70
    (d) $90

31. What is the power consumed by a 10 kW heat strip rated 230V connected to an 115V circuit?

    (a) 2.50 kW
    (b) 5 kW
    (c) 7.50 kW
    (d) 15 kW

CHAPTER 3—BASIC ELECTRICAL CIRCUITS

UNIT 10—SERIES CIRCUITS

32. The opposition to current flow results in voltage drop.

    (a) True
    (b) False

33. Kirchoff's Voltage Law states, "In a series circuit, the sum of the voltage drops across all of the resistors will equal the applied voltage."

    (a) True
    (b) False

34. Kirchoff's Current Law states, "In a series circuit, the current is _____ through the transformer, the conductors, and the appliance."

    (a) proportional
    (b) distributed
    (c) additive
    (d) the same

UNIT 11—PARALLEL CIRCUITS

35. According to Kirchoff's Current Law, the total current provided by the source to a parallel circuit will equal the sum of the currents of all of the branches.

    (a) True
    (b) False

36. The total resistance of a parallel circuit can be calculated by the _____ method.

    (a) equal resistance
    (b) product-over-sum
    (c) reciprocal
    (d) any of these

37. When power supplies are connected in parallel, the voltage remains the same, but the current or amp-hour capacity will be increased.

    (a) True
    (b) False

UNIT 13—MULTIWIRE CIRCUITS

38. A balanced 3-wire, 120/240V, single-phase circuit is connected so that the ungrounded conductors are from different transformer phases (Line 1 and Line 2). The current on the neutral conductor will be _____ percent of the ungrounded conductor current.

    (a) 0
    (b) 70
    (c) 80
    (d) 100

39. If the ungrounded conductors of a multiwire circuit are not terminated to different phases, this can cause the neutral current to be in excess of the neutral conductor rating.

    (a) True
    (b) False

40. The current flowing on the neutral conductor of a multiwire circuit is called "unbalanced current."

    (a) True
    (b) False

41. Improper wiring or mishandling of multiwire branch circuits can cause _____ connected to the circuit.

    (a) overloading of the ungrounded conductors
    (b) overloading of the neutral conductors
    (c) destruction of equipment because of overvoltage
    (d) b and c

42. Because of the dangers associated with an open neutral conductor, the continuity of the _____ conductor cannot be dependent upon the receptacle.

    (a) ungrounded
    (b) grounded
    (c) a and b
    (d) none of these

CHAPTER 4— ELECTRICAL SYSTEMS AND PROTECTION

UNIT 14—THE ELECTRICAL SYSTEM

43. Electrons leaving a power supply are always trying to return to the same power supply; they are not trying to go into the earth.

    (a) True
    (b) False

44. To prevent fires and electric shock, the *NEC* specifies that neutral current can flow on metal parts of the electrical system.

    (a) True
    (b) False

45. Metal parts of premises wiring must be bonded to a low-impedance path designed so that the circuit protection device will quickly open and clear a ground fault.

    (a) True
    (b) False

46. Because of the earth's high resistance to current flow, it cannot be used for the purpose of clearing a line-to-case ground fault for _____ wiring.

    (a) utility
    (b) premises
    (c) a or b
    (d) none of these

UNIT 15—PROTECTION DEVICES

Part A—Overcurrent Protection Devices

47. The purpose of overcurrent protection is to protect the conductors and equipment against excessive or dangerous temperatures because of overcurrent. Overcurrent is current in excess of the rated current of equipment or conductors. It may result from a(n) _____.

    (a) overload
    (b) short circuit
    (c) ground fault
    (d) all of these

48. To protect against electric shock or to prevent a fire, a dangerous _____ must quickly be removed by opening the circuit's overcurrent protection device.

    (a) overload
    (b) short circuit
    (c) ground fault
    (d) all of these

49. Inverse time breakers operate on the principle that as the current decreases, the time it takes for the device to open decreases.

    (a) True
    (b) False

50. The _____ sensing element causes the circuit breaker to open when a predetermined calibration temperature is reached.

    (a) magnetic
    (b) electronic
    (c) thermo
    (d) none of these

51. The magnetic time-delay circuit breaker operates on the solenoid principle where a movable core, held with a spring, is moved by the magnetic field of a(n) _____.

    (a) overload
    (b) short circuit
    (c) ground fault
    (d) b or c

52. Available short-circuit current is the current in amperes available at a given point in the electrical system.

    (a) True
    (b) False

53. Factors that affect the available short-circuit current include transformer _____.

    (a) voltage
    (b) kVA rating
    (c) impedance
    (d) all of these

54. Factors that affect the available short-circuit current include circuit conductor _____.

    (a) material
    (b) size
    (c) length
    (d) all of these

55. Circuit breakers and fuses are intended to interrupt the circuit, and they must have an ampere interrupting rating (AIR) sufficient for the available short-circuit current.

    (a) True
    (b) False

56. If the protection device is not rated to interrupt the current at the available fault values at its listed voltage rating, it can explode while attempting to clear the fault.

    (a) True
    (b) False

57. Equipment must have a(n) _____ current rating that permits the protection device to clear a short circuit or ground fault without extensive damage to the components of the circuit.

    (a) overload
    (b) short-circuit
    (c) ground-fault
    (d) b or c

Part B—Ground-Fault Circuit Interrupters

58. A GFCI is designed to protect persons against electric shock. It operates on the principle of monitoring the imbalance of current between the circuit's _____ conductor.

    (a) ungrounded
    (b) grounded
    (c) equipment
    (d) a and b

59. A GFCI-protection device contains an internal monitor that prevents the device from being turned on if there is a neutral-to-case connection downstream of the device, but this only occurs if there is a load on the circuit.

    (a) True
    (b) False

60. Severe electric shock or death can occur if a person touches the ungrounded and the neutral conductors at the same time, even if the circuit is GFCI-protected.

    (a) True
    (b) False

61. Typically, when a GFCI-protection device fails, the switching contacts remain closed and the device will continue to provide power without GFCI protection.

    (a) True
    (b) False

Part C—Arc-Fault Circuit Interrupters

62. Arcing is defined as a luminous discharge of electricity across an insulating medium. Electric arcs operate at temperatures between _____ and expel small particles of very hot molten material.

    (a) 1,000 and 5,000°F
    (b) 2,000 and 10,000°F
    (c) 5,000 and 15,000°F
    (d) 10,000 and 25,000°F

63. Unsafe arcing faults can occur in one of two ways, as series arcing faults or as parallel arcing faults. The most dangerous is the parallel arcing fault.

    (a) True
    (b) False

64. An AFCI-protection device provides protection from an arcing fault by recognizing the characteristics unique to an arcing fault and by functioning to de-energize the circuit when an arc fault is detected.

    (a) True
    (b) False

CHAPTER 5—ALTERNATING CURRENT

UNIT 16—ALTERNATING CURRENT

65. A nonsinusoidal waveform is created when _____ loads distort the voltage and current sine wave.

    (a) linear
    (b) resistive
    (c) inductive
    (d) nonlinear

66. When describing the relationship between voltage and current, the reference waveform is always _____.

    (a) current
    (b) resistance
    (c) voltage
    (d) none of these

67. The effective value is equal to the peak value _____.

    (a) times 0.707
    (b) times 1.41
    (c) times 2
    (d) times $\sqrt{3}$

UNIT 17—CAPACITANCE

68. Even when power is removed from the circuit, capacitors can store large amounts of energy for a long period of time. They can discharge and arc if inadvertently shorted or grounded out.

    (a) True
    (b) False

69. The opposition offered to the flow of ac current by a capacitor is called "capacitive reactance," which is expressed in ohms and abbreviated _____.

    (a) X_c
    (b) X_L
    (c) Z
    (d) none of these

UNIT 18—INDUCTION

70. The induced voltage in a conductor carrying alternating current opposes the change in current flowing through the conductor. The induced voltage that opposes the current flow is called "_____."

    (a) CEMF
    (b) counter-electromotive force
    (c) back-EMF
    (d) all of these

71. For ac circuits, the ac _____ of a conductor must be taken into consideration.

    (a) eddy currents
    (b) skin effect
    (c) resistance
    (d) all of these

72. The expanding and collapsing magnetic field within the conductor induces a voltage in the conductors (CEMF) that repels the flowing electrons toward the surface of the conductor. This is called "_____."

    (a) eddy currents
    (b) induced voltage
    (c) impedance
    (d) skin effect

73. The total opposition to current flow in ac circuits is called "_____" and measured in ohms.

    (a) resistance
    (b) reactance
    (c) impedance
    (d) skin effect

74. The abbreviation for impedance is _____.

    (a) X_L
    (b) X_C
    (c) Z
    (d) none of these

75. Self-induced voltage opposes the change in current flowing in the conductor. This is called "inductive reactance" and it is abbreviated _____.

    (a) X_L
    (b) X_C
    (c) Z
    (d) none of these

UNIT 19—POWER FACTOR AND EFFICIENCY

Part A—Power Factor

76. AC inductive or capacitive reactive loads cause the voltage and current to be in-phase with each other.

    (a) True
    (b) False

77. What size transformer is required for a 100A, 240V, single-phase noncontinuous load that has a power factor of 85 percent?

    (a) 15 kVA
    (b) 25 kVA
    (c) 37.50 kVA
    (d) 50 kVA

78. How many 20A, 120V circuits are required for forty-two, 300W luminaires (noncontinuous load) that have a power factor of 85 percent?

    (a) 4 circuits
    (b) 5 circuits
    (c) 7 circuits
    (d) 8 circuits

Part B—Efficiency

79. If the output is 1,600W and the equipment is 88 percent efficient, what are the input amperes at 120V?

    (a) 10A
    (b) 15A
    (c) 20A
    (d) 25A

CHAPTER 6—MOTORS, GENERATORS, AND TRANSFORMERS

UNIT 20—MOTORS

Part A—Motor Basics

80. Dual-voltage ac motors are made with two field windings. The field windings are connected in _____ for low-voltage operation and in _____ for high-voltage operation.

    (a) series, parallel
    (b) parallel, series
    (c) series, series
    (d) parallel, parallel

81. The motor FLA rating is used when sizing motor conductor size or circuit protection.

    (a) True
    (b) False

82. What is the nameplate FLA for a 20 hp, 208V, three-phase motor with 90 percent power factor and 80 percent efficiency?

    (a) 51A
    (b) 58A
    (c) 65A
    (d) 80A

83. When a motor starts, the current drawn is approximately _____ times the motor FLA; this is known as "motor locked-rotor amperes" (LRA).

    (a) 0.80
    (b) 1.25
    (c) 3
    (d) 6

84. If the rotating part of the motor winding is jammed so that it cannot rotate, no CEMF will be produced in the motor winding. Result—the motor operates at _____ and the windings will be destroyed by excessive heat.

    (a) FLA
    (b) FLC
    (c) LRC
    (d) any of these

85. In an ac induction motor, the stator produces a rotating magnetic field that induces current in the rotor windings. The rotor current generates a magnetic field in opposition to the magnetic field of the stator, thereby causing the rotor to turn.

    (a) True
    (b) False

86. In a(n) _____ motor, the rotor is locked in step with the rotating stator field and is dragged along at the speed of the rotating magnetic field.

    (a) wound-rotor
    (b) induction
    (c) synchronous
    (d) squirrel-cage

87. _____ motors are fractional horsepower motors that operate equally well on ac and dc and are used for vacuum cleaners, electric drills, mixers, and light household appliances.

    (a) AC
    (b) Universal
    (c) Wound-rotor
    (d) Synchronous

88. Swapping _____ of the line conductors can reverse a three-phase ac motor's rotation.

    (a) one
    (b) two
    (c) three
    (d) four

89. The _____ of an ac generator contains the electromagnetic field, which cuts through the stationary conductor coils.

    (a) stator
    (b) rotor
    (c) coil
    (d) winding

90. Three-phase ac generators have three equally spaced windings, _____ out-of-phase with each other.

    (a) 90°
    (b) 120°
    (c) 180°
    (d) 360°

91. The energy transfer ability of a transformer is accomplished because the primary electromagnetic lines of force induce a voltage in the secondary winding.

    (a) True
    (b) False

92. Voltage induced in the secondary winding of a transformer is dependent on the number of secondary turns as compared to the number of primary turns.

    (a) True
    (b) False

93. Wasteful circulating _____ in the iron core cause(s) the core to heat up without any useful purpose.

    (a) conductor resistance
    (b) flux leakage
    (c) eddy currents
    (d) hysteresis losses

94. _____ can be reduced by dividing the core into many flat sections or laminations.

    (a) Conductor resistance
    (b) Flux leakage
    (c) Eddy currents
    (d) Hysteresis losses

95. As current flows through the transformer, the iron core is temporarily magnetized. The energy required to realign the core molecules to the changing electromagnetic field is called "_____" loss.

    (a) conductor resistance
    (b) flux leakage
    (c) eddy currents
    (d) hysteresis

96. Three-phase, _____, wye-connected systems can overheat because of circulating odd triplen harmonic currents.

    (a) 2-wire
    (b) 3-wire
    (c) 4-wire
    (d) none of these

97. The heating from harmonic currents is proportional to the square of the harmonic current.

    (a) True
    (b) False

98. Because of conductor resistance, flux leakage, eddy currents, and hysteresis losses, not all of the input power is transferred to the secondary winding for useful purposes.

    (a) True
    (b) False

99. If the primary phase voltage is 480V and the secondary phase voltage is 240V, the turns ratio is _____.

    (a) 1:2
    (b) 1:41
    (c) 2:1
    (d) 4:1

100. Transformers are rated in _____.

    (a) VA
    (b) kW
    (c) W
    (d) kVA

Suggested Study Materials:

Only when you truly know electrical theory can you have confidence in the practical aspects of your electrical work. **Mike Holt's Basic Electrical Theory program** will give you the foundation you need to pass this portion of your exam. This library includes DVDs and *Mike Holt's Illustrated Guide to Basic Electrical Theory* and will help you understand what electricity is, how it is used and how it is produced. You will learn everything from a brief study of matter to a breakdown of circuits for controls, fire alarms, security and much more. You will also learn the basics for motors and transformers. The full-color textbook provides hundreds of illustrated graphics, detailed examples, practice questions and more to break down this topic for you.

Visit www.MikeHolt.com/Theory or call 888.632.2633.

Notes

Mike Holt's Journeyman Simulated Exam, based on the 2014 NEC

Please use the 2014 Code book to answer the following questions. If you need a copy of the *Code* book, visit www.MikeHolt.com/14Code or call 888.632.2633

1. Wiring methods used in health care locations must comply with the *NEC* Chapter 1 through 4 provisions, except as modified by Article 517.

   (a) True
   (b) False

2. All 15A and 20A, single-phase, 125V through 250V receptacles located within _____ ft of a fountain edge shall have GFCI protection.

   (a) 8
   (b) 10
   (c) 15
   (d) 20

3. General purpose Type CL2, CM, or CATV cables are permitted within the raised floor area of an information technology equipment room.

   (a) True
   (b) False

4. Type AC cable installed through, or parallel to, framing members shall be protected against physical damage from penetration by screws or nails.

   (a) True
   (b) False

5. For a sign, outline lighting system, or skeleton tubing system, the equipment grounding conductor size shall be in accordance with _____, based on the rating of the overcurrent device protecting the conductors supplying the sign or equipment.

   (a) 250.66
   (b) 250.122
   (c) 310.13
   (d) 310.16

6. When installing PVC conduit underground without concrete cover, there shall be a minimum of _____ in. of cover.

   (a) 6
   (b) 12
   (c) 18
   (d) 22

7. Unused openings other than those intended for the operation of equipment, intended for mounting purposes, or permitted as part of the design for listed equipment shall be _____.

   (a) filled with cable clamps or connectors only
   (b) taped over with electrical tape
   (c) repaired only by welding or brazing in a metal slug
   (d) closed to afford protection substantially equivalent to the wall of the equipment

8. Overhead service conductors can be supported to hardwood trees.

   (a) True
   (b) False

9. Complete raceway systems of underground PVC can be located less than 5 ft from the inside wall of a pool when space limitations are encountered and shall be buried not less than _____ in. with at least 4 in. of concrete cover.

   (a) 6
   (b) 10
   (c) 12
   (d) 18

10. In judging equipment for approval, considerations such as the following shall be evaluated:

    (a) mechanical strength
    (b) wire-bending space
    (c) arcing effects
    (d) all of these

11. Rigid metal conduit that is directly buried outdoors shall have at least _____ in. of cover.

    (a) 6
    (b) 12
    (c) 18
    (d) 24

12. A(n) _____ system is an electrical source, other than a service, having no direct connection(s) to circuit conductors of any other electrical source other than those established by grounding and bonding connections.

    (a) separately derived
    (b) classified
    (c) direct
    (d) emergency

13. Alternating-current general-use snap switches are permitted to control _____.

    (a) resistive and inductive loads that do not exceed the ampere and voltage rating of the switch
    (b) tungsten-filament lamp loads that do not exceed the ampere rating of the switch at 120V
    (c) motor loads that do not exceed 80 percent of the ampere and voltage rating of the switch
    (d) all of these

14. Electrical equipment rooms or enclosures housing electrical apparatus that are controlled by a lock(s) shall be considered _____ to qualified persons.

    (a) readily accessible
    (b) accessible
    (c) available
    (d) none of these

15. Duct heater controller equipment shall have a disconnecting means installed within _____ the controller except as allowed by 424.19(A).

    (a) 25 ft of
    (b) sight from
    (c) the side of
    (d) none of these

16. Optical fiber cables not terminated at equipment, and not identified for future use with a tag are considered abandoned.

    (a) True
    (b) False

17. Overcurrent devices for legally required standby systems shall be _____ with all supply-side overcurrent devices.

    (a) series rated
    (b) selectively coordinated
    (c) installed in parallel
    (d) any of these

18. Acceptable protection techniques for electrical and electronic equipment in hazardous (classified) locations includes:

    (a) Explosionproof Equipment
    (b) Dust Ignitionproof
    (c) Dusttight
    (d) all of these

19. A 15A or 20A, 125V receptacle outlet shall be located within 25 ft of heating, air-conditioning, and refrigeration equipment for _____ occupancies.

    (a) dwelling
    (b) commercial
    (c) industrial
    (d) all of these

20. EMT shall not be used where _____.

    (a) subject to severe physical damage
    (b) protected from corrosion only by enamel
    (c) used for the support of luminaires
    (d) any of these

21. Unlisted conductive and nonconductive outside plant optical fiber cables shall be permitted to be installed in locations other than risers, ducts used for environmental air, plenums used for environmental air, and other spaces used for environmental air, where the length of the cable within the building, measured from its point of entrance, does not exceed _____ ft and the cable enters the building from the outside and is terminated in an enclosure.

    (a) 25
    (b) 50
    (c) 75
    (d) 100

22. Type NM cables shall not be used in one- and two-family dwellings exceeding three floors above grade.

    (a) True
    (b) False

23. Utilization equipment weighing not more than 6 lb can be supported to any box or plaster ring secured to a box, provided the equipment is secured with at least two _____ or larger screws.

    (a) No. 6
    (b) No. 8
    (c) No. 10
    (d) self tapping

24. Concrete, brick, or tile walls are considered _____, as applied to working space requirements.

    (a) inconsequential
    (b) in the way
    (c) grounded
    (d) none of these

25. Grounding electrodes of the rod type less than _____ in diameter shall be listed.

    (a) ½ in.
    (b) ⅝ in.
    (c) ¾ in.
    (d) none of these

26. Luminaires and equipment must be mechanically connected to an equipment grounding conductor as specified in 250.118 and must be sized in accordance with _____.

    (a) Table 250.66
    (b) Table 250.122
    (c) Table 310.16
    (d) a and c

27. In Division 1 or Division 2 locations where the boxes, fittings, or enclosures are required to be explosionproof, if a flexible cord is used it must terminate with a cord connector or attachment plug listed for the location, or a listed cord connector installed with a seal that is listed for the location. In Division 2 locations where explosionproof equipment is not required, the cord shall terminate _____.

    (a) with a listed cord connector
    (b) with a listed attachment plug
    (c) in a splice of any manner
    (d) a or b

28. FMC shall be supported and secured _____.

    (a) at intervals not exceeding 4½ ft
    (b) within 8 in. on each side of a box where fished
    (c) where fished
    (d) at intervals not exceeding 6 ft

29. Article 501 covers the requirements for electrical and electronic equipment and wiring for all voltages in Class I locations where fire or explosion hazards may exist due to flammable _____.

    (a) gases
    (b) vapors
    (c) liquids
    (d) any of these

30. Where the Class I, Division 1 location boundary is below grade, a sealing fitting shall be permitted to be installed _____, and there must not be any unions, couplings, boxes, or fittings between the sealing fitting and the grade, other than listed explosionproof reducers.

    (a) after the conduit emerges from grade
    (b) before the conduit emerges from grade
    (c) within 10 ft of where the conduit emerges from grade
    (d) none of these

31. Lighting track fittings can be equipped with general-purpose receptacles.

    (a) True
    (b) False

32. The grounding electrode conductor for a single separately derived system is used to connect the grounded conductor of the derived system to the grounding electrode.

    (a) True
    (b) False

33. Receptacle outlets installed for a specific appliance in a dwelling unit, such as laundry equipment, shall be located within _____ of the intended location of the appliance.

    (a) sight
    (b) 3 ft
    (c) 6 ft
    (d) none of these

34. A load is considered to be continuous if the maximum current is expected to continue for _____ or more.

    (a) one-half hour
    (b) 1 hour
    (c) 2 hours
    (d) 3 hours

35. Two or more grounding electrodes bonded together are considered a single grounding electrode system.

    (a) True
    (b) False

36. Where RMC enters a box, fitting, or other enclosure, _____ shall be provided to protect the wire from abrasion, unless the design of the box, fitting, or enclosure affords equivalent protection.

    (a) a bushing
    (b) duct seal
    (c) electrical tape
    (d) seal fittings

37. Equipment grounding conductors for motor branch circuits shall be sized in accordance with Table 250.122, based on the rating of the _____ device.

    (a) motor overload
    (b) motor over-temperature
    (c) branch-circuit short-circuit and ground-fault protective
    (d) feeder overcurrent protection

38. "Varying duty" is defined as _____.

    (a) intermittent operation in which the load conditions are regularly recurrent
    (b) operation at a substantially constant load for an indefinite length of time
    (c) operation for alternate intervals of load and rest, or load, no load, and rest
    (d) operation at loads, and for intervals of time, both of which may be subject to wide variation

39. Access to electrical equipment shall not be denied by an accumulation of communications _____ that prevents the removal of suspended-ceiling panels.

    (a) wires
    (b) cables
    (c) ductwork
    (d) a and b

40. Alternating-current systems of 50V to 1,000V that supply premises wiring systems shall be grounded where supplied by a three-phase, 4-wire, delta-connected system in which the midpoint of one phase winding is used as a circuit conductor.

    (a) True
    (b) False

41. The recommended maximum total voltage drop on branch-circuit conductors is _____ percent.

    (a) 2
    (b) 3
    (c) 4
    (d) 6

42. In one- and two-family dwellings where it is not practicable to achieve an overall maximum primary protector grounding electrode conductor length of 20 ft, a separate ground rod not less than _____ ft shall be driven and it shall be connected to the power grounding electrode system with a 6 AWG conductor.

    (a) 5
    (b) 8
    (c) 10
    (d) 20

43. _____, 125V and 250V receptacles installed in a wet location shall have an enclosure that is weatherproof whether or not the attachment plug cap is inserted.

    (a) 15A
    (b) 20A
    (c) a and b
    (d) none of these

44. The requirement to maintain a 3-foot vertical clearance from the edge of a roof does not apply to the final conductor span where the service drop is attached to _____.

    (a) a service pole
    (b) the side of a building
    (c) an antenna
    (d) the base of a building

45. The armor of Type AC cable containing an aluminum bonding strip is recognized by the NEC as an equipment grounding conductor.

    (a) True
    (b) False

46. A separate portion of a raceway system that provides access through a removable cover(s) to the interior of the system, defines the term _____.

    (a) junction box
    (b) accessible raceway
    (c) conduit body
    (d) cutout box

47. Article _____ covers the installation of portable wiring and equipment for carnivals, circuses, exhibitions, fairs, traveling attractions, and similar functions.

    (a) 518
    (b) 525
    (c) 590
    (d) all of these

48. Where the circuit breaker handles are operated vertically, the up position of the handle shall be the _____ position.

    (a) on
    (b) off
    (c) tripped
    (d) any of these

49. Switches shall not be installed within tubs or shower spaces unless installed as part of a listed tub or shower assembly.

    (a) True
    (b) False

50. Snap switches, including dimmer and similar control switches, shall be connected to an equipment grounding conductor and shall provide a means to connect metal faceplates to the equipment grounding conductor, whether or not a metal faceplate is installed.

    (a) True
    (b) False

51. In Class III locations, receptacles and attachment plugs shall be of the grounding type, shall be designed so as to minimize the accumulation or the entry of _____, and shall prevent the escape of sparks or molten particles.

    (a) gases or vapors
    (b) particles of combustion
    (c) fibers/flyings
    (d) none of these

52. For optional standby systems, the temporary connection of a portable generator without transfer equipment shall be permitted where conditions of maintenance and supervision ensure that only qualified persons will service the installation, and where the normal supply is physically isolated by _____.

    (a) a lockable disconnecting means
    (b) the disconnection of the normal supply conductors
    (c) an extended power outage
    (d) a or b

53. Communications equipment includes equipment and conductors used for the transmission of _____.

    (a) audio
    (b) video
    (c) data
    (d) any of these

54. Wiring from an emergency source can emergency or other loads, provided the conductors _____.

    (a) terminate in separate vertical sections of a switchboard
    (b) terminate in the same vertical section of a switchboard
    (c) terminate in a junction box identified for emergency use
    (d) are identified as emergency conductors

55. When applying the general provisions for receptacle spacing to the rooms of a dwelling unit which require receptacles in the wall space, no point along the floor line in any wall space of a dwelling unit may be more than _____ from an outlet.

    (a) 6 ft
    (b) 8 ft
    (c) 10 ft
    (d) 12 ft

56. For grounded systems, electrical equipment and electrically conductive material likely to become energized, shall be installed in a manner that creates a low-impedance circuit capable of safely carrying the maximum ground-fault current likely to be imposed on it from where a ground fault may occur to the _____.

    (a) ground
    (b) earth
    (c) electrical supply source
    (d) none of these

57. There shall be no reduction in the size of the neutral or grounded conductor on _____ loads supplied from a 4-wire, wye-connected, three-phase system.

    (a) dwelling unit
    (b) hospital
    (c) nonlinear
    (d) motel

58. An emergency system shall have adequate capacity and rating for _____ to be operated simultaneously.

    (a) 80% of the loads
    (b) all loads
    (c) 125% of the load
    (d) none of these

59. A pool light junction box connected to a conduit that extends directly to a forming shell shall be _____ for this use.

    (a) listed
    (b) identified
    (c) marked
    (d) a and b

60. Each portable structure at a carnival, circus, or fair shall be provided with a means to disconnect it from all ungrounded conductors within sight of and within _____ ft of the operator's station.

    (a) 3
    (b) 6
    (c) 8
    (d) 10

61. In dwelling units, all nonlocking type 125V, 15A and 20A receptacles installed _____ shall be listed as tamper resistant.

    (a) in bedrooms
    (b) outdoors, at grade level
    (c) above counter tops
    (d) in all areas specified in 210.52, except as covered by exceptions

62. GFCI protection shall be required for all 125V receptacles not exceeding 30A and located within 6 ft measured _____ from the inside walls of a hydromassage bathtub.

    (a) vertically
    (b) horizontally
    (c) across
    (d) none of these

63. In multi-occupancy buildings, branch circuits for _____ shall not be supplied from equipment that supplies an individual dwelling unit or tenant space.

    (a) a central alarm
    (b) parking lot lighting
    (c) common area purposes
    (d) all of these

64. Vegetation such as trees shall not be used for support of _____.

    (a) overhead conductor spans
    (b) surface wiring methods
    (c) luminaires
    (d) electric equipment

65. Limiting the length of the primary protector grounding conductors for communications circuits helps to reduce voltage between the building's _____ and communications systems during lightning events.

    (a) power
    (b) fire alarm
    (c) lighting
    (d) lightning protection

66. Nonmetallic boxes can be used with _____.

    (a) nonmetallic sheaths
    (b) nonmetallic raceways
    (c) flexible cords
    (d) all of these

67. A feeder supplying fixed motor load(s) shall have a protective device with a rating or setting _____ branch-circuit short-circuit and ground-fault protective device for any motor in the group, plus the sum of the full-load currents of the other motors of the group.

    (a) not greater than the largest rating or setting of the
    (b) 125 percent of the largest rating of any
    (c) equal to the largest rating of any
    (d) none of these

68. When 15A and 20A receptacles are installed in a wet location, the outlet box _____ must be listed for extra-duty use.

    (a) sleeve
    (b) hood
    (c) threaded entry
    (d) mounting

69. A _____ shall be located in sight from the motor location and the driven machinery location.

    (a) controller
    (b) protection device
    (c) disconnecting means
    (d) all of these

70. As used in the *NEC*, equipment includes _____.

    (a) fittings
    (b) appliances
    (c) machinery
    (d) all of these

71. Receptacles installed outdoors, in a location protected from the weather or other damp locations, shall be in an enclosure that is _____ when the receptacle is covered.

    (a) raintight
    (b) weatherproof
    (c) rainproof
    (d) weathertight

72. For wiring methods, "on or attached to the surface, or behind access panels designed to allow access" is known as _____.

    (a) open
    (b) uncovered
    (c) exposed
    (d) bare

73. In industrial facilities where conditions of maintenance and supervision ensure that only qualified persons will service the installation, cable tray systems can be used to support _____.

    (a) raceways
    (b) cables
    (c) boxes and conduit bodies
    (d) all of these

74. Where flammable liquids having a flash point below 100°F (such as gasoline), or gaseous fuels such as natural gas or hydrogen, will not be transferred in a minor repair garage, such location is considered to be a(n) _____ location, provided the entire floor area has mechanical ventilation providing a minimum of four air changes per hour or one cubic foot per minute of exchanged air for each square foot of floor area.

    (a) Class I, Division 1
    (b) Class I, Division 2
    (c) Class II, Division 1
    (d) unclassified

75. Where a luminaire stud or hickey is present in the box, a _____ volume allowance in accordance with Table 314.16(b) shall be made for each type of fitting, based on the largest conductor present in the box.

    (a) single
    (b) double
    (c) single allowance for each gang
    (d) none of these

76. For stationary motors of 2 hp or less and 300V or less on ac circuits, the controller can be an ac-rated only general-use snap switch where the motor full-load current rating is not more than _____ percent of the rating of the switch.

    (a) 50
    (b) 60
    (c) 70
    (d) 80

77. In major repair garages where lighter-than-air gaseous fueled vehicles, such as vehicles fueled by natural gas or hydrogen, are repaired or stored, the area within _____ in. of the ceiling is classified as Class I, Division 2.

    (a) 6
    (b) 12
    (c) 18
    (d) 24

78. Article 600 covers the installation of conductors, equipment, and field wiring for _____.

    (a) electric signs
    (b) outline lighting
    (c) neon tubing
    (d) all of these

79. The minimum clearance for overhead service conductors not exceeding 600V that pass over commercial areas subject to truck traffic is _____ ft.

    (a) 10
    (b) 12
    (c) 15
    (d) 18

80. Short-circuit and ground-fault protection for an individual air-conditioner motor-compressor shall not exceed _____ percent of the motor-compressor rated-load current or branch-circuit selection current, whichever is greater.

    (a) 80
    (b) 125
    (c) 175
    (d) 250

81. Fountain equipment supplied by a flexible cord shall have all exposed noncurrent-carrying metal parts grounded by an insulated copper equipment grounding conductor that is an integral part of the cord.

    (a) True
    (b) False

82. Grounding electrode conductor taps from a separately derived system to a common grounding electrode conductor are permitted when a building or structure has multiple separately derived systems, provided that the taps terminate at the same point as the system bonding jumper.

    (a) True
    (b) False

83. An overload is the same as a short circuit or ground fault.

    (a) True
    (b) False

84. A box shall not be required where cables or conductors from cable trays are installed in bushed conduit and tubing used as support or for protection against _____.

    (a) abuse
    (b) unauthorized access
    (c) physical damage
    (d) tampering

85. Flexible cords used in Class II, Division 1 or 2 locations shall _____, except as permitted for pendant luminaires .

    (a) be listed for hard usage
    (b) be listed for extra-hard usage
    (c) not be permitted
    (d) none of these

86. A written record shall be kept of required tests and maintenance on emergency systems.

    (a) True
    (b) False

87. A nursing home is an area used for the housing and nursing care, on a 24-hour basis, of _____ or more persons who, because of mental or physical incapacity, might be unable to provide for their own needs and safety without the assistance of another person.

    (a) two
    (b) three
    (c) four
    (d) five

88. An unspliced _____ that is sized based on the derived phase conductors shall be used to connect the grounded conductor and the supply-side bonding jumper, or the equipment grounding conductor, or both, at a separately derived system.

    (a) system bonding jumper
    (b) equipment grounding conductor
    (c) grounded conductor
    (d) grounding electrode conductor

89. A circuit breaker with a _____ voltage rating, such as 240V or 480V, can be used where the nominal voltage between any two conductors does not exceed the circuit breaker's voltage rating.

    (a) straight
    (b) slash
    (c) high
    (d) low

90. Track lighting shall not be installed _____.

    (a) where likely to be subjected to physical damage
    (b) in wet or damp locations
    (c) a and b
    (d) none of these

91. Optical fiber cables shall not be _____ to the exterior of any conduit or raceway as a means of support.

    (a) strapped
    (b) taped
    (c) attached
    (d) all of these

92. Where livestock is housed, any portion of an underground equipment grounding conductor run to the building or structure shall be _____.

    (a) insulated
    (b) covered
    (c) either a or b
    (d) neither a nor b

93. If a protective device rating is marked on an appliance, the branch-circuit overcurrent device rating shall not exceed _____ percent of the protective device rating marked on the appliance.

    (a) 50
    (b) 80
    (c) 100
    (d) 115

94. Attachment plugs and cord connectors shall be listed and marked with the _____.

    (a) manufacturer's name or identification
    (b) voltage rating
    (c) amperage rating
    (d) all of these

95. Type S fuses, fuseholders, and adapters shall be designed so that _____ would be difficult.

    (a) installation
    (b) tampering
    (c) shunting
    (d) b or c

96. Receptacles shall not be grouped or ganged in enclosures unless the voltage between adjacent devices does not exceed _____.

    (a) 100V
    (b) 200V
    (c) 300V
    (d) 400V

97. The common point on a wye-connection in a polyphase system describes a neutral point.

    (a) True
    (b) False

98. Grommets or bushings for the protection of Type NM cable shall be _____ for the purpose.

    (a) marked
    (b) approved
    (c) identified
    (d) listed

99. The term "Luminaire" includes an individual lampholder.

    (a) True
    (b) False

100. Which of the following is not a standard size fuse or inverse time circuit breaker?

    (a) 45A
    (b) 70A
    (c) 75A
    (d) 80A

Mike Holt's Journeyman Simulated Exam, based on the 2014 NEC

PART 3

ELECTRICAL CALCULATIONS EXAM (5 HOURS)

The questions in this part relate directly to *Mike Holt's Illustrated Guide to Electrical Exam Preparation* textbook.

CHAPTER 1—ELECTRICAL THEORY

UNITS 1 THROUGH 4— ELECTRICAL THEORY

Figure 1 applies to Questions 1 through 3.

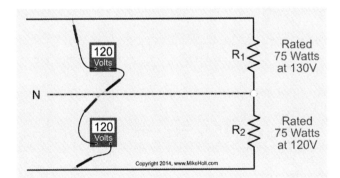

Figure 1

1. The resistance of R_1 is _____.

   (a) 19.20 ohms
   (b) 22.50 ohms
   (c) 192 ohms
   (d) 225 ohms

2. The current of Lamp 2 (R_2) is _____ amperes.

   (a) 0.54
   (b) 0.63
   (c) 5.40
   (d) 6.30

3. The total power consumed of both circuits combined will be _____ watts.

   (a) 139
   (b) 150
   (c) 278
   (d) 300

Figure 2 applies to Questions 4 and 5.

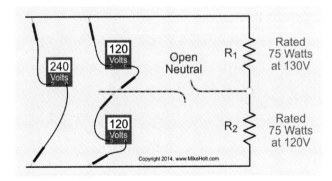

Figure 2

4. If the neutral path is opened as shown in Figure 2, the current of the circuit will be _____ amperes.

   (a) 0.58
   (b) 0.63
   (c) 0.93
   (d) a and b

5. If the neutral is open as shown in Figure 2, what is the voltage drop across the 120V rated bulb (R$_2$)?

    (a) 110V
    (b) 115V
    (c) 120V
    (d) 240V

Figure 3 applies to Questions 6 through 10:

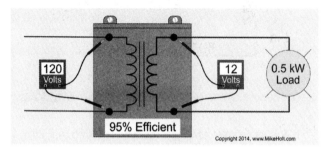

Figure 3

6. The secondary power is closest to _____ VA.

    (a) 475
    (b) 500
    (c) 526
    (d) 550

7. If this transformer is 100 percent efficient, the primary current will be _____ amperes.

    (a) 3.56
    (b) 4.16
    (c) 4.39
    (d) 4.42

8. The primary power is closest to _____ VA.

    (a) 475
    (b) 500
    (c) 526
    (d) 550

9. The primary current of the transformer is approximately _____ amperes, at 95 percent efficiency.

    (a) 0.416
    (b) 3.56
    (c) 4.32
    (d) 4.38

10. The resistance of the load can be found by the formula R = _____.

    (a) E^2/P
    (b) E^2/I
    (c) P/I
    (d) I^2R

Figure 4 applies to Questions 11 and 12.

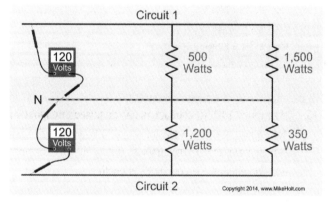

Figure 4

11. The resistance of a 500W, 120V load is approximately _____ ohms.

    (a) 9.60
    (b) 12
    (c) 20
    (d) 28.80

12. What is the total load of Circuit 1?

    (a) 500 watts
    (b) 1,500 watts
    (c) 2,000 watts
    (d) 3,200 watts

CHAPTER 2—*NEC* CALCULATIONS

UNIT 5—RACEWAY AND BOX CALCULATIONS

13. Can a round 4 x ½ in. box marked as 8 cu in. with manufactured cable clamps supplied with 14/2 NM be used with a luminaire that has two 18 AWG fixture wires and a canopy cover?

    (a) Yes
    (b) No

14. What size outlet box is required for one 12/2 NM cable that terminates on a switch, one 12/3 NM cable that terminates on a receptacle, and the box has manufactured cable clamps?

    (a) 4 x 1¼ square
    (b) 4 x 1½ square
    (c) 4 x 2⅛ square
    (d) none of these

15. How many 14 AWG conductors can be pulled through a 4 x 1½ square box with a plaster ring of 3.60 cu in.? The box contains two duplex receptacles, five 14 AWG conductors, and two equipment grounding conductors.

    (a) 1
    (b) 2
    (c) 3
    (d) 4

The following information applies to Questions 16 through 18: A junction box has two trade size 3 raceways entering on the left side. The conductors from one of these leave the top of the box in a trade size 3 raceway in an angle pull. The conductors from the second trade size 3 on the left wall are pulled straight through one of the trade size 2 raceways on the right. Two trade size 2 raceways enter from the right side and two trade size 3 raceways enter from the bottom. All raceways entering the bottom are angle pulls. Figure 5

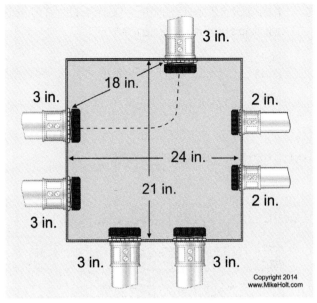

Figure 5

16. What is the distance from the left wall to the right wall?

    (a) 18 in.
    (b) 20 in.
    (c) 21 in.
    (d) 24 in.

17. What is the distance from the bottom wall to the top wall?

    (a) 15 in.
    (b) 18 in.
    (c) 21 in.
    (d) 24 in.

18. What is the distance between the raceways that contain the same conductors?

    (a) 15 in.
    (b) 18 in.
    (c) 21 in.
    (d) 24 in.

19. How many 16 TFFN conductors can be installed in trade size ¾ electrical metallic tubing?

    (a) 26
    (b) 29
    (c) 30
    (d) 40

20. How many 1/0 XHHW conductors can be installed in a trade size 2 flexible metal conduit?

    (a) 6
    (b) 7
    (c) 13
    (d) 16

21. If we have a trade size 2 rigid metal conduit and we want to install three THHN compact conductors, what is the largest compact conductor permitted to be installed?

    (a) 4/0 AWG
    (b) 250 kcmil
    (c) 350 kcmil
    (d) 500 kcmil

22. What is the cross-sectional area in sq in. for 10 THW?

    (a) 0.0172
    (b) 0.0243
    (c) 0.0252
    (d) 0.0278

23. What is the cross-sectional area in sq in. for an 8 AWG bare solid conductor?

    (a) 0.013
    (b) 0.027
    (c) 0.038
    (d) 0.045

24. A 200A feeder installed in Schedule 40 rigid nonmetallic conduit has three 3/0 THHN, one 2 THHN, and one 6 THHN. What trade size raceway is required?

    (a) 2
    (b) 2½
    (c) 3
    (d) 3½

25. What trade size rigid metal nipple is required for three 4/0 THHN, one 1/0 THHN, and one 4 THHN?

    (a) 1½
    (b) 2
    (c) 2½
    (d) 3

26. An existing trade size ¾ rigid metal nipple contains four 10 THHN and one 10 AWG (bare stranded) ground wire. How many additional 10 THHN conductors can be installed?

    (a) 5
    (b) 7
    (c) 9
    (d) 11

UNIT 6—CONDUCTOR SIZING AND PROTECTION

27. A 2 TW conductor is installed in a location where the ambient temperature is expected to be 102°F. The temperature correction factor for conductor ampacity in this location is _____.

    (a) 0.71
    (b) 0.82
    (c) 0.88
    (d) 0.96

28. The ampacity of six current-carrying 4/0 XHHW aluminum conductors installed in a ground floor slab (wet location) is _____.

    (a) 135A
    (b) 144A
    (c) 185A
    (d) 210A

29. The ampacity of 15 current-carrying 10 RHW aluminum conductors in an ambient temperature of 75°F is _____.

    (a) 12A
    (b) 16A
    (c) 22A
    (d) 30A

30. A(n) _____ THHN conductor is required for a 19.70A load if the ambient temperature is 75°F and there are nine current-carrying conductors in the raceway.

    (a) 8
    (b) 10
    (c) 12
    (d) 14

31. The ampacity of nine current-carrying 10 THW conductors installed in a 20 in. long raceway is _____.

    (a) 25A
    (b) 30A
    (c) 35A
    (d) 40A

UNIT 7—VOLTAGE-DROP CALCULATIONS

32. What is the ac ohms-to-neutral resistance for 100 ft of 3 AWG copper conductor?

    (a) 0.012 ohms
    (b) 0.025 ohms
    (c) 0.33 ohms
    (d) 0.43 ohms

33. A 24A, 240V, single-phase load is located 160 ft from the panelboard. The load is wired with 10 AWG conductors. What is the approximate voltage drop of the branch-circuit conductors?

    (a) 3.20V
    (b) 4.25V
    (c) 5.90V
    (d) 9.50V

34. A single-phase, 5 hp motor is located 110 ft from a panelboard. The nameplate indicates that the voltage is 115/230V and the FLA is 52/26A. What size conductor is required if the motor windings are connected to operate at 115V? Apply the *NEC* recommended voltage-drop limits.

    (a) 10 AWG
    (b) 8 AWG
    (c) 6 AWG
    (d) 3 AWG

35. What is the approximate distance that a single-phase, 7.50 kVA, 240V load can be located from the panelboard so the voltage drop does not exceed 3 percent? The load is wired with 8 AWG copper.

    (a) 55 ft
    (b) 110 ft
    (c) 145 ft
    (d) 220 ft

36. An existing installation consists of 1/0 AWG copper conductors in a nonmetallic raceway to a panelboard located 200 ft from a single-phase, 240V power source. What is the maximum load that can be placed on the panelboard so that the *NEC* recommendations for voltage drop are not exceeded?

    (a) 71A
    (b) 94A
    (c) 109A
    (d) 147A

UNIT 8—MOTOR AND AIR-CONDITIONING CALCULATIONS

37. What size conductor is required for a 5 hp, 230V, single-phase motor? The terminals are rated 75°C.

    (a) 14 AWG
    (b) 12 AWG
    (c) 10 AWG
    (d) 8 AWG

38. Motors with a nameplate service factor (SF) rating of 1.15 or more must have the overload device sized at no more than _____ percent of the motor nameplate current rating.

    (a) 100
    (b) 115
    (c) 125
    (d) 135

39. Motors with a nameplate temperature rise rating not over 40°C must have the overload device sized at no more than _____ percent of motor nameplate current rating.

    (a) 100
    (b) 115
    (c) 125
    (d) 135

40. If a dual-element fuse is used for overload protection, what size fuse is required for a 5 hp, 208V, three-phase motor with a service factor of 1.16, and a motor nameplate current rating of 16A (FLA)?

    (a) 20A
    (b) 25A
    (c) 30A
    (d) 35A

41. Which of the following statements are true for a 10 hp, 208V, three-phase motor with a nameplate current of 29A?

    (a) The branch-circuit conductors can be 8 AWG
    (b) Overload protection is 33A
    (c) Short-circuit and ground-fault protection can be an 80A circuit breaker
    (d) all of these

42. What is the VA input of a dual voltage 5 hp, three-phase motor rated 460/230V?

    (a) 3,027 VA at 460V
    (b) 6,055 VA at 230V
    (c) 6,055 VA at 460V
    (d) b and c

43. The branch-circuit conductors of a 5 hp, 230V motor with a nameplate rating of 25A must have an ampacity of not less than _____. *Note: The motor is used for intermittent duty and, due to the nature of the apparatus it drives, it cannot run for more than five minutes at any one time.*

    (a) 21A
    (b) 23A
    (c) 33A
    (d) 37A

44. The standard overload protection device for a 2 hp, 115V motor that has a full-load current rating of 24A and a nameplate rating of 21.50A must not exceed _____.

    (a) 20.60A
    (b) 24.70A
    (c) 29.90A
    (d) 33.80A

45. The ultimate trip overload device of a thermally protected 1½ hp, 115V motor would be rated no more than _____.

    (a) 23A
    (b) 26A
    (c) 28A
    (d) 31.20A

46. A 2 hp, 115V motor requires a _____ branch-circuit short-circuit protection device. *Note: Use an inverse time breaker for protection.*

    (a) 20A
    (b) 30A
    (c) 40A
    (d) 60A

UNIT 9—DWELLING UNIT CALCULATIONS

The following information applies to Questions 47 through 51: Laundry circuit of 1,500 VA; two small-appliance circuits are 3,000 VA; ½ hp, 115V motor. Balance these loads on a 115/230V single-phase system, then answer questions 47 through 51.

47. What is the VA of the ½ hp, 115V motor?

    (a) 1,127 VA
    (b) 1,176 VA
    (c) 2,254 VA
    (d) 2,688 VA

48. The total panel load is _____ VA.

    (a) 1,127
    (b) 3,000
    (c) 4,500
    (d) 5,627

49. The total current of both Line 1 and Line 2 equals _____ amperes.

    (a) 30–35
    (b) 36–40
    (c) 41–45
    (d) 46–50

50. The neutral current will be _____ amperes if all loads are on.

    (a) 0 (zero)
    (b) 3
    (c) 10
    (d) 15

51. Under the most severe conditions, the neutral will carry _____ amperes.

    (a) 18.20
    (b) 20
    (c) 23
    (d) 26

52. Balance the following loads and determine the load on the neutral in amperes.

    3,000 VA, 120V small appliance
    1,500 VA, 120V laundry circuit
    1,800 VA, 120V dishwasher
    2,000 VA, 240V dryer
    1,500 VA, 120V disposal.

    (a) 0 (zero)A
    (b) 2.50A
    (c) 3.50A
    (d) 10A

53. What is the feeder/service calculated load for one 6 kW and two 3 kW cooking appliances?

    (a) 4.50 kW
    (b) 4.80 kW
    (c) 6 kW
    (d) 9.30 kW

54. What is the feeder/service calculated load for an 11.50 kW range?

    (a) 6 kW
    (b) 8 kW
    (c) 9.20 kW
    (d) 11.50 kW

55. What is the feeder/service calculated load for a 13.60 kW range?

    (a) 6 kW
    (b) 8 kW
    (c) 8.80 kW
    (d) 9.20 kW

56. How many 15A general-lighting circuits are required for a 2,340 sq ft home?

    (a) 2
    (b) 3
    (c) 4
    (d) 5

57. What is the total calculated load for general lighting and receptacles, and small-appliance and laundry circuits for a 6,540 sq ft dwelling unit before applying demand factors?

    (a) 2,700 VA
    (b) 8,100 VA
    (c) 12,600 VA
    (d) 24,120 VA

58. What is the feeder/service calculated load for one air conditioner (5 hp, 230V) and three baseboard heaters (3 kW)?

    (a) 3,000 VA
    (b) 5,400 VA
    (c) 8,050 VA
    (d) 9,000 VA

59. What is the feeder/service calculated load for a waste disposal (940 VA), dishwasher (1,250 VA), and a water heater (4,500 VA)?

    (a) 5,018 VA
    (b) 6,272 VA
    (c) 6,690 VA
    (d) 8,363 VA

60. What is the feeder/service calculated load for a 4 kW dryer?

    (a) 3 kW
    (b) 4 kW
    (c) 5 kW
    (d) 6 kW

61. What AWG size copper conductors are required for the single-phase 120/240V feeder/service conductors for a dwelling unit with a 190A service calculated load?

    (a) 1/0 AWG
    (b) 2/0 AWG
    (c) 3/0 AWG
    (d) 4/0 AWG

62. The feeder/service neutral load for household cooking appliances such as electric ranges, wall-mounted ovens, or counter-mounted cooking units must be calculated at _____ percent of the calculated load as determined by 220.55.

    (a) 50
    (b) 60
    (c) 70
    (d) 80

63. Both units of a duplex apartment require a 100A main; the resulting 200A service will require _____ copper conductors.

    (a) 1/0 AWG
    (b) 2/0 AWG
    (c) 3/0 AWG
    (d) 4 AWG

64. An 1,800 sq ft residence contains the following: a 4 kW water heater, one 1.50 kW dishwasher, one 4.50 kW dryer, two 3 kW ovens, one 6 kW range, 10 kW of space heat separated in five rooms with thermostats in each room, and one 6 kVA air conditioner. The 120/240V single-phase service for the loads will be _____ when using the optional method of calculation.

    (a) 110A
    (b) 125A
    (c) 150A
    (d) 175A

65. After balancing the following loads, what is the maximum unbalanced neutral current?

    Three 1,900W, 120V lighting loads, and two 2 hp, 115V motors.

    (a) 48A
    (b) 54A
    (c) 57A
    (d) 65A

Notes

1. (a) True

2. (a) True

3. (b) False

4. (b) False

5. (b) False

6. (b) False

7. (a) True

8. (a) True

9. (a) True

10. (d) 30,000° F

11. (a) True

12. (d) magnetic

13. (d) resistance

14. (d) resistance

15. (d) magnetic

16. (b) rotor

17. (b) False

18. (a) True

19. (a) True

20. (a) True

21. (b) False

22. (b) False

23. (c) 6.40V

$$E = I \times R$$

E = 16A x 0.40 ohms

E = 6.40V

24. (a) 0.14 ohms

$$R = E/I$$

R = 7.20V/50A

R = 0.14 ohms

25. (a) 175W

$$P = I \times E$$

P = 24A x 7.20V

P = 172.80W

26. (a) 8.20 kW

The power of the heat strip will be less because the applied voltage (208V) is less than the equipment voltage rating (230V). To calculate this, we must determine the heat strip resistance rating at 230V, and then determine the power rating at 208V based on the heat strip resistance rating.

$$P = E^2/R$$

E = Applied Voltage = 208V

R = Resistance of Heat Strip = E^2/P

Heat Strip Voltage Rating = 230V

Power Rating of Heat Strip = 10,000W

Resistance of Heat Strip = $230V^2/10,000W$

Resistance of Heat Strip = 5.29 ohms

$$P = E^2/R$$

P = (208V x 208V)/5.29 ohms

P = 43,624/5.29 ohms

P = 8,178W/1,000

P = 8.20 kW

27. (d) a and b

28. (b) 100W

$$P = I^2 \times R$$

I = 16A

R = 0.40 ohms

P = (16A x 16A) x 0.40 ohms

P = 102.40W

29. (a) 43W

$P = I \times E$
I = 12A
E = 120V x 3%
E = 3.60V
P = 12A x 3.60V
P = 43.20W

30. (c) $70

Cost per Year = Power for the Year in kWh x $0.08
Power per Hour = I^2 x R
I = 16A
R = 0.40 ohms

Power per Hour = (16A x 16A) x 0.40 ohms
Power per Hour = 102.40W
Power for the Year in kWh = (102.40W x 24 hours x 365 days)/1,000
Power for the Year in kWh = 897 kWh

Cost per Year = 897 kWh x $0.08
Cost per Year = $71.76

31. (a) 2.50 kW

The power of the heat strip will be less because the applied voltage (115V) is less than the equipment voltage rating (230V). To calculate this, we must determine the heat strip resistance rating at 230V, and then determine the power rating at 115V based on the heat strip resistance rating.

$P = E^2/R$
E = Applied Voltage = 115V
R = Resistance of Heat Strip = E^2/P
Heat Strip Voltage Rating = 230V

Power Rating of Heat Strip = 10,000W
Resistance of Heat Strip = $230V^2/10,000W$
Resistance of Heat Strip = 5.29 ohms

$P = E^2/R$
P = 13,225/5.29 ohms
P = 2,500W/1,000 = 2.50 kW

Note: Power changes with the square of the voltage. If the voltage is reduced to 50%, then the power consumed will be equal to the new voltage percent² or 50%², or 10,000 x (0.50 x 0.50 = 0.25 = 25%) = 2,500W = 2.50 kW.

32. (a) True

33. (a) True

34. (d) the same

35. (a) True

36. (d) any of these

37. (a) True

38. (a) 0

39. (a) True

40. (a) True

41. (d) b and c

42. (b) grounded

43. (a) True

44. (b) False

45. (a) True

46. (b) premises

47. (d) all of these

48. (d) all of these

49. (b) False

50. (c) thermo

51. (d) b or c

52. (a) True

53. (d) all of these

54. (d) all of these

55. (a) True

56. (a) True

57. (b) short-circuit

58. (d) a and b

59. (b) False

60. (a) True

61. (a) True

62. (c) 5,000 and 15,000° F

63. (a) True

64. (a) True

65. (d) nonlinear

66. (c) voltage

67. (a) times 0.707

68. (a) True

69. (a) X_c

70. (d) all of these

71. (d) all of these

72. (d) skin effect

73. (c) impedance

74. (c) Z

75. (a) X_L

76. (b) False

77. (b) 25 kVA

Transformer kVA = (Volts x Amperes)/1,000
Transformer kVA = (240V x 100A)/1,000
Transformer kVA = 24

Note: The power factor value given in the question has nothing to do with determining the kVA of a load.

78. (c) 7 circuits

VA per Circuit = Volts x Amperes
VA per Circuit = 120V x 20A
VA per Circuit = 2,400 VA

VA per Luminaire = Watts/Power Factor
VA per Luminaire = 300W/0.85 PF
VA per Luminaire = 353 VA

Lights per Circuit = 2,400 VA/353 VA = 6.80
Lights per Circuit = 6
Circuits = 42 luminaires/6 per circuit
Circuits = 7

79. (b) 15A

Input Watts = Output Watts/Efficiency
Input = 1,600W/0.88 Eff
Input = 1,818W
Input Amperes = Watts/Volts
Input Amperes = 1,818W/120V
Input Amperes = 15.167A

80. (b) parallel, series

81. (b) False

82. (b) 58A

FLA = (Motor hp x 746W)/(E x 1.732 x PF x Eff)
FLA = (20 hp x 746W)/(208V x 1.732 x 0.9 PF x 0.80 Eff)
FLA = 58A

83. (d) 6

84. (c) LRC

85. (a) True

86. (c) synchronous

87. (b) Universal

88. (b) two

89. (b) rotor

90. (b) 120°

91. (a) True

92. (a) True

93. (c) eddy currents

94. (c) Eddy currents

95. (d) hysteresis

96. (c) 4-wire

97. (a) True

98. (a) True

99. (c) 2:1

100. (d) kVA

Notes

Mike Holt's Journeyman Simulated Exam, based on the 2014 NEC

Question	Answer	*NEC* Section #
1.	(a)	517.12 and 90.3
2.	(d)	680.58
3.	(a)	645.5(E)(6)c. and Table 645.5(E)(6)
4.	(a)	320.17
5.	(b)	600.7(A)(2)
6.	(c)	300.5(A) and Table 300.5 Column 3
7.	(d)	110.12(A)
8.	(b)	230.10
9.	(a)	680.10 and Table 680.10
10.	(d)	110.3(A)(2), (3), and (6)
11.	(a)	300.5(A) and Table 300.5 Column 2
12.	(a)	100 Separately Derived System
13.	(d)	404.14(A)(1), (2), and (3)
14.	(b)	110.26(F)
15.	(b)	424.65
16.	(a)	770.2 Abandoned Optical Fiber Cable
17.	(b)	701.27
18.	(d)	500.7(A), (B), and (C)
19.	(d)	210.63
20.	(d)	358.12(1), (2), and (5)
21.	(b)	770.48(A)
22.	(b)	334.10(1)
23.	(a)	314.27(D) Ex
24.	(c)	110.26(A)(1) and Table 110.26(A)(1), Condition 2
25.	(b)	250.52(A)(5)(b)
26.	(b)	410.44
27.	(d)	501.140(B)(4)
28.	(a)	348.30(A)
29.	(d)	501.1

Question	Answer	*NEC* Section #
30.	(a)	501.15(A)(4) Ex 2
31.	(b)	410.151(A)
32.	(a)	250.30(A)(5)
33.	(c)	210.50(C)
34.	(d)	100 Continuous Load
35.	(a)	250.53(B) and 250.58
36.	(a)	344.46
37.	(c)	250.122(D)(1)
38.	(d)	100 Duty, Varying
39.	(d)	800.21
40.	(a)	250.20(B)(3)
41.	(b)	210.19(A) Note 4
42.	(a)	800.100(A)(4) Ex and 800.100(B)(3)(2)
43.	(c)	406.9(B)(1)
44.	(b)	230.24(A) Ex 4
45.	(a)	250.118(8)
46.	(c)	100 Conduit Body
47.	(b)	525.1
48.	(a)	240.81
49.	(a)	404.4(C)
50.	(a)	404.9(B)
51.	(c)	503.145
52.	(d)	702.5 Ex
53.	(d)	100 Communications Equipment
54.	(a)	700.10(B)(5)a
55.	(a)	210.52(A)(1)
56.	(c)	250.4(A)(5)
57.	(c)	220.61(C)(2)
58.	(b)	700.4(A)

Question	Answer	*NEC* Section #
59.	(a)	680.24(A)(1)
60.	(b)	525.21(A)
61.	(d)	406.12(A)
62.	(b)	680.71
63.	(d)	210.25(B)
64.	(a)	225.26
65.	(a)	800.100(A)(4) Note
66.	(d)	314.3
67.	(a)	430.62(A)
68.	(b)	406.9(B)(1)
69.	(c)	430.102(B)(1)
70.	(d)	100 Equipment
71.	(b)	406.9(A)
72.	(c)	100 Exposed (as applied to wiring methods)
73.	(d)	392.18(G)
74.	(d)	511.3(D)(1)(a)
75.	(a)	314.16(B)(3)
76.	(d)	430.83(C)(2)
77.	(c)	511.3(C)(2)(a) and (b)
78.	(d)	600.1
79.	(d)	230.24(B)(4)

Question	Answer	*NEC* Section #
80.	(c)	440.22(A)
81.	(a)	680.55(B)
82.	(a)	250.30(A)(6)
83.	(b)	100 Overload
84.	(c)	392.46
85.	(b)	502.140(B)(1)
86.	(a)	700.3(D)
87.	(c)	517.2 Nursing Home
88.	(a)	250.30(A)(1)
89.	(a)	240.85
90.	(c)	410.151(C)(1) and (2)
91.	(d)	770.133(D)
92.	(b)	547.5(F)
93.	(c)	422.11(A) and 422.10(A)
94.	(d)	406.7
95.	(d)	240.54(D)
96.	(c)	406.5(H)
97.	(a)	100 Neutral Point
98.	(d)	334.17
99.	(b)	100 Luminaire
100.	(c)	240.6(A)

Note: The calculations are shown immediately following the answers. Methods other than the ones we used may be correct in some cases. If you used a different method of calculation to come up with the same answer, it's probably okay.

1. (d) 225 ohms

    R_1 = Voltage Rating of Lamp²/Power Rating of Lamp
    $R_1 = 130V^2/75W$
    $R_1 = 225$ ohms

2. (b) 0.63

    I_2 = Voltage Rating of Lamp/Resistance Rating of Lamp
    $E = 120V$
    R_2 = Voltage Rating²/Power Rating
    $R_2 = 120V^2/75W$
    $R_2 = 192$ ohms
    $I_2 = E/R_2$
    $I_2 = 120V/192$ ohms
    $I_2 = 0.625A$, rounded to 0.63A

    Reminder: A multiwire circuit with a common neutral is treated as two separate series circuits.

3. (a) 139

    Power Total = $P_1 + P_2$
    $P_1 = E^2/R$
    $P_1 = 120V^2/225$ ohms
    $P_1 = 64W$
    $P_2 = 75W$
    Power Total = 64W + 75W
    Power Total = 139W

Figure 6 applies to Answers 4 and 5:

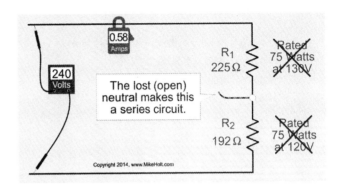

Figure 6

4. (a) 0.58

    If neutral is open, the multiwire circuit becomes a 240V series circuit. The current of the circuit is equal to $I = E/R$.

    E = 240V series circuit
    R_1 = 225 ohms (answer key question 1)
    R_2 = 192 ohms (answer key question 2)
    I = 240V/(225 ohms + 192 ohms)
    I = 240V/417 ohms
    I = 0.575A, rounded to 0.58A

5. (a) 110V

    The voltage across the 120V rated light bulb R_2 is equal to $E_2 = I_T \times R_2$.
    I_T = Voltage Source/Resistance Total
    I_T = 240V/417 ohms (answer key question 4)
    $I_T = 0.575A$
    $E_2 = I_T \times R_2$
    $E_2 = 0.575A \times 192$ ohms
    $E_2 = 110V$

6. (b) 500

   Secondary Power 0.50 kVA x 1,000 = 500 VA

7. (b) 4.16

   If 100% efficient, the Primary VA is 500.
   Primary Current = Primary VA/Primary E
   Primary Current = 500 VA/120V = 4.16A

8. (c) 526

   Primary Power = Secondary VA/Efficiency
   Primary Power = 500 VA/0.95
   Primary Power = 526 VA

9. (d) 4.38

   Primary Current = Primary VA/Primary Volts
   Primary Current = 526 VA/120V
   Primary Current = 4.38A

10. (a) E^2/P

11. (d) 28.80 ohms

    $R = E^2/P$
    $R = 120V^2/500W$
    R = 28.80 ohms

12. (c) 2,000 watts

    500 watts + 1,500 watts = 2,000 watts

13. (a) Yes

    The exception to 314.16(B)(1) permits us to omit fixture wires that enter the outlet box from a luminaire canopy.

    Step 1: Determine the number and size of conductors:

14/2 NM cable	2 – 14 AWG
Ground wire	1 – 14 AWG
One cable clamp	1 – 14 AWG

    Step 2: Volume of the conductors [Table 314.16(B)]:

    4 conductors x 2 cu in. = 8.00 cu in.

14. (c) 4 x 2⅛ square

    Step 1: Determine the number and size of conductors:

12/2 NM cable	2 – 12 AWG conductors
12/3 NM cable	3 – 12 AWG conductors
Cable clamps	1 – 12 AWG conductors
Switch	2 – 12 AWG conductors
Receptacles	2 – 12 AWG conductors
Ground wire	1 – 12 AWG conductor
Total Number	11 – 12 AWG conductors

    Step 2: Determine the volume (cubic inches) of the above conductors [Table 314.16(B)]:

    11 conductors x 2.25 = 24.75 cu in.

    Step 3: Select the outlet box from Table 314.16(A):

    4 x 2⅛ in. square = 30.30 cu in.

15. (b) 2

    Step 1: Determine the number and size of the existing conductors:

Two receptacles	4 – 14 AWG conductors
Five 14 AWG	5 – 14 AWG conductors
Two ground wires	1 – 14 AWG conductor
Total Conductors	10 – 14 AWG conductors

    Step 2: Determine the volume of the existing conductors [Table 314.16(B)]:

    10 conductors x 2 cu in. = 20 cu in.

    Step 3: Determine the spare space area:

    A. 4 x 1½ square box = 21 cu in. + 3.60 cu in. (ring) = 24.60 cu in.
    B. Spare Space:
       24.60 cu in. – 20 cu in. = 4.60 cu in.

    Step 4: 14 AWG conductors permitted in spare space: Spare Space/Conductor Volume:

    4.60 cu in./2 cu in. = 2 conductors [Table 314.16(B)]

Figure 7 applies to Answers 16 through 18:

16. (d) 24 in., [314.28(A)]

    Left wall to right wall angle pull: (6 x 3) + 3 = 21 in.
    Left wall to right wall straight pull: 8 x 3 = 24 in.
    Right wall to left wall angle pull: (6 x 2) + 2 = 14 in.
    Right wall to left wall straight pull: 8 x 2 = 16 in.

17. (c) 21 in., [314.28(A)]

    Bottom wall to top wall angle pull: (6 x 3) + 3 = 21 in.
    Bottom wall to top wall straight pull: No calculation
    Top wall to bottom wall angle pull: 6 x 3 = 18 in.
    Top wall to bottom wall straight pull: No calculation

18. (b) 18 in., [314.28(A)(2)]

    6 x 3 = 18 in.

19. (b) 29, [Annex C, Table C.1]

20. (b) 7, [Annex C, Table C.3]

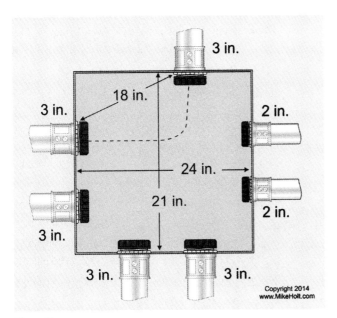

Figure 7

21. (c) 350 kcmil, [Annex C, Table C.8(A)]

22. (b) 0.0243, [Chapter 9, Table 5]

23. (a) 0.013, [Chapter 9, Table 8]

   8 AWG Solid = 0.013 sq in.
   8 AWG Stranded = 0.017 sq in.

24. (a) 2

   Step 1: Area of the conductors [Chapter 9, Table 5]:

   3 – 3/0 THHN: 0.2679 sq in. x 3 = 0.8037 sq in.
   1 – 2 THHN: 0.1158 sq in. x 1 = 0.1158 sq in.
   1 – 6 THHN: 0.0507 sq in. x 1 = 0.0507 sq in.

   Step 2: Total square inch area of the conductors:
   0.9702 sq in.

   Step 3: Permitted conductor fill at 40% fill: [Chapter 9,
   Table 1 and Table 4]

   Trade size 2 Schedule 40 PVC area in 40%
   column = 1.316 sq in.

25. (a) 1½

   Step 1: Find the square inch area of the conductors
   [Chapter 9, Table 5].

   3 – 4/0 THHN: 0.3237 sq in. x 3 =0.9711 sq in.
   1 – 1/0 THHN: 0.1855 sq in. x 1 = 0.1855 sq in.
   1 – 4 THHN: 0.0824 sq in. x 1 = 0.0824 sq in.

   Step 2: Total square inch area of the conductors: 1.239
   sq in.

   Step 3: Size the conduit at 60% fill [Chapter 9, Table 4,
   Note 3]

   Trade size 1¼: 0.916 sq in.—Too Small
   Trade size 1½: 1.243 sq in.—Just Right
   Trade size 2: 2.045 sq in.—Larger Than Needed

26. (d) 11

   Step 1: Area of conductor fill permitted for a trade size
   ¾ nipple – Chapter 9, Table 4: 0.329 sq in.

   Step 2: Square inch area of the existing conductors
   [Chapter 9, Table 5]:

   4–10 THHN: 0.0211 sq in. x 4 = 0.0844 sq in.
   1–10 AWG bare stranded [Chapter 9, Table 8]:
   0.0110 sq in. x 1 = 0.0110 sq in.

   Total area of existing conductors = 0.0954 sq in.

   Step 3: Subtract the area of the existing conductors
   from the area of permitted conductor fill:

   Spare Space Area:
   Permitted Area Fill less Existing Conductors Area
   Spare Space Area = 0.3290 sq in. –0.0954 sq in.
   Spare Space Area = 0.2336 sq in.

   Step 4: Determine the number of 10 THHN conductors
   that can be added to the available spare space:

   Number of conductors permitted: Spare Space
   Area/Area of Conductors
   Number of 10 THHN conductors permitted:
   0.2336 sq in. /0.0211
   Number of conductors permitted = 11 conductors

27. (b) 0.82, Table 310.15(B)(16).

   Bottom, 60°C wire at 102°F. Be sure to use a straight
   edge when using a table!

28. (b) 144A, [310.15(B)(3)(a) and Table 310.15(B)(2)(a)]

   Ampacity = Table Ampacity x Bundling Adjustment
   Table 310.15(B)(16) Ampacity: 4/0 XHHW aluminum in a
   wet location = 180A*
   Six current-carrying conductors factor = 0.80
   Ampacity = Table Ampacity x Bundling Adjustment
   Ampacity = 180A x 0.80 = 144A

   *Note: Table 310.104(A) requires that when XHHW is
   used in a wet location, we must use the 75°C ampacity
   column of Table 310.15(B)(16). See definition of "Location, Wet".*

29. (b) 16A, [310.15(B)(3)(a) and Table 310.15(B)(2)(a)]

    Ampacity = Amperes x Temperature Correction x Bundling Adjustment

    Table 310.15(B)(16) Ampacity: 10 RHW aluminum = 30A at 75°C

    Temperature Correction: 75°C wire at 75°F = 1.05
    15 current-carrying conductors factor = 0.50
    Ampacity = 30A x 1.05 x 0.50 = 15.75A

30. (c) 12, [310.15(B)(3)(a) and Table 310.15(B)(2)(a)]

    Ampacity = Amperes x Temperature Correction x Bundling Adjustment

    Table ampacity:
    14 THHN – 25A at 90°C
    12 THHN – 30A at 90°C
    10 THHN – 40A at 90°C
    8 THHN – 55A at 90°C

    Ambient Temperature Correction: 90°C wire at 75°F = 1.04 [Table 310.15(B)(2)(a)]

    9 current-carrying conductors adjustment = 0.70 [Table 310.15(B)(3)(a)]

    14 THHN Ampacity = 25A x 1.04 x 0.70 = 18.20A
    12 THHN Ampacity = 30A x 1.04 x 0.70 = 21.84A

31. (c) 35A

    Bundling factors do not apply to raceways that are 24 in. in length or less (nipples) [310.15(B)(3)(a)(2)]

    Table 310.15(B)(16) Ampacity: 10 AWG THW at 75°C = 35A

32. (b) 0.025 ohms, [Chapter 9, Table 9]

    (0.25 ohms/1,000) ft x 100 ft = 0.025 ohms

33. (d) 9.50V

    VD = (2 x K x I x D)/Cmil
    K = 12.90 ohms, copper
    I = 24A
    D = 160 ft
    Cmil of 10 AWG = 10,380 Cmil [Table 8, Chapter 9]
    VD = (2 x 12.90 ohms x 24A x 160 ft)/10,380 Cmil
    VD = 9.50V

34. (d) 3 AWG

    Cmil = (2 x K x I x D)/VD
    K = 12.90 ohms, copper
    I = 52A, not FLC
    D = 110 ft
    VD = 3.45V (115V x 0.03) [210.19 (A)(1) FPN No. 4]
    Cmil = (2 x 12.90 ohms x 52A x 110 ft)/3.45V
    Cmil = 42,776 Cmil
    Chapter 9, Table 8 = 3 AWG

35. (c) 145 ft

    D = (Cmil x VD)/(2 x K x Q x I)
    Cmil = 16,510 Cmil
    VD = 240V x 0.03
    VD = 7.20V
    K = 12.90 ohms
    Q = Less than 2/0 AWG, does not apply

    I = VA/V
    I = 7,500 VA/240V
    I = 31.25A

    D = (16,510 Cmil x 7.20V)/(2 x 12.90 ohms x 31.25A)
    D = 118,872/806
    D = 147 or approximately 145 ft

    Note: Do not confuse distance (D) with length (L). This formula gives the distance between two points, not the length of conductors in the run.

36. (d) 147A

    I = (Cmil x VD)/(2 x K x D)
    Cmil of 1/0 AWG = 105,600 Cmil [Chapter 9, Table 8]
    VD = 240V x 0.03
    VD = 7.20V
    K = 12.90 ohms, copper
    D = 200 ft
    I = (105,600 Cmil x 7.20V)/(2 x 12.90 ohms x 200 ft)
    I = 760,320/5,160
    I = 147A

    Note: The maximum load permitted on 1/0 THHN is 150A at 75°C, 110.14(C)(2) and Table 310.15(B)(16).

37. (c) 10 AWG

    The FLC for a 5 hp motor = 28A [Table 430.248]
    28A x 1.25 = 35A [430.22(A)]
    10 AWG at 75°C is rated 35A [Table 310.15(B)(16)]

38. (c) 125, [430.32(A)(1)]

39. (c) 125, [430.32(A)(1)]

40. (a) 20A, [430.32(A)(1) and 430.6(A)(2)]

Overloads are sized according to the nameplate current rating, not the motor FLC 16A x 1.25 = 20A.

41. (d) All of these

FLC = 30.80A [Table 430.250]

Conductor [430.22(A)]: 30.80A x 1.25 = 38.50A

8 AWG is rated 40A at 60ªC [Table 310.15(B)(16)]

Overload protection [430.32(A)(1)]: 29A (nameplate) x 1.15 = 33A

Short-circuit and ground-fault protection [430.52]: 30.80A (FLC) x 2.50 = 77A, next size up circuit breaker = 80A [430.52(C)(1) Ex 1]

42. (d) b and c

5 hp, 460V three-phase FLC = 7.60A
5 hp, 230V three-phase FLC = 15.20A
[Table 430.250]
VA of 5 hp motor at 460V =
  460V x 7.60A x 1.732 = 6,055 VA
VA of 5 hp motor at 230V =
  230V x 15.20A x 1.732 = 6,055 VA

43. (a) 21A, [430.22(E) and Table 430.22(E)]

The branch-circuit conductor ampacity must not be less than 85% of the motor nameplate amperes. Table 430.22(E) Intermittent and 5-minute rated motor: 25A x 0.85 = 21.25A.

44. (b) 24.70A, [430.32(A)(1)]

The motor overload for this motor must be sized no more than 115% of the motor nameplate current rating: 21.50A x 1.15 = 24.73A

45. (d) 31.20A, [430.32(A)(2) and Table 430.248]

1½ hp, 115V motor has a FLC of 20A [Table 430.248]

The ultimate trip device must be sized not more than 156% of the motor FLC rating!

430.32(A)(2): 20A x 1.56 = 31.20A

46. (d) 60A

2 hp 115V FLC = 24A [Table 430.248]

The branch-circuit protection device shall not be greater than 250% of the motor FLC. [430.52(C)(1) and Table 430.52]: 24A x 2.50 = 60A

47. (a) 1,127 VA

½ hp at 115V FLC = 9.80A [Table 430.248]
Motor VA = Volts x Amperes
Motor VA = 115V x 9.80A
½ hp Motor VA = 1,127 VA

48. (d) 5,627 VA

	L1	L2
Small-Appliance Circuits	1,500 VA	1,500 VA
Laundry Circuit	1,500 VA	
½ hp Motor		1,127 VA
	3,000 VA	2,627 VA

Total VA Load = 3,000 VA + 2,627 VA
Total VA Load = 5,627 VA

49. (d) 46-50

Line 1 = 3,000 VA/115V
Line 1 = 26A
Line 2 = 2,627 VA/115V
Line 2 = 22.80A

Total Current = Line 1 + Line 2
Total Current = 26A + 22.80A
Total Current = 48.80A

50. (b) 3

Neutral Load = 3,000 VA – 2,627 VA
Neutral Load = 373 VA
Neutral Current = VA/E
Neutral Current = 373 VA/115V
Neutral Current = 3.24A, or
Neutral Current = L1 – L2

Line 1 Current = 3,000 VA/115V =	26.10A
Line 2 Current = 2,627 VA/115V =	– 22.80A
Neutral Current	3.30A

51. (d) 26

3,000 VA/115V = 26A

52. (d) 10A

	L1	L2
Small-Appliance Circuit	1,500 VA	1,500 VA
Laundry Circuit	1,500 VA	
Dishwasher		1,800 VA
Disposal	1,500 VA	
	4,500 VA	3,300 VA

Neutral Load = 4,500 VA – 3,300 VA
Neutral Load = 1,200 VA

Neutral Current = VA/E
Neutral Current = 1,200 VA/120V
Neutral Current = 10A, or
Neutral Current = L1 – L2

Line 1 Current = 4,500 VA/120V =	37.50A
Line 2 Current = 3,300 VA/120V =	– 27.50A
Neutral Current	10.00A

53. (d) 9.30 kW
[Table 220.55]

Column B: 6 kW x 0.80 =	4.80 kW
Column A: 3 kW x 2 units = 6 kW x 0.75 =	4.50 kW
Calculated Load	9.30 kW

54. (b) 8 kW, [Table 220.55]

Column C: 8 kW

55. (c) 8.80 kW

The Column C value (8 kW) must be increased 5% for each kW or major fraction of a kW (0.50 kW or larger) over 12 kW.

13.60 kW – 12 kW = 1.60
2 x 5% = 10%
8 kW x 1.10 = 8.80 kW

56. (c) 4

Step 1: General Lighting VA:

3 VA / sq ft [Table 220.12]
2,340 sq ft x 3 VA = 7,020 VA

Step 2: General Lighting Amperes: I = VA/E

I = 7,020 VA/120V
I = 58.50A

Step 3: Determine the number of circuits:

Circuits = General Lighting Amperes/Circuit Amperes
Circuits = 58.50/15
Circuits = 3.93 or 4

Note: Use 120 or 120/240V, single-phase unless specified otherwise [220.5(A)]

57. (d) 24,120 VA

General lighting and receptacles

6,540 sq ft x 3 VA =	19,620 VA
Small-appliance circuits 1,500 VA x 2 =	3,000 VA
Laundry circuit 1,500 VA x 1 =	+ 1,500 VA
Calculated Load	24,120 VA

58. (d) 9,000 VA

A/C, 230V 5 hp FLC = 28A [Table 430.248]
VA = V x A
VA = 230V x 28A
VA = 6,440 VA*
Heat: 3,000 VA x 3 = 9,000 VA [220.51]
*Omit the smaller of the two loads [220.60].

59. (c) 6,690 VA

Disposal	940 VA
Dishwasher	1,250 VA
Water heater	+ 4,500 VA
	6,690 VA

[220.53]

60. (c) 5 kW

The dryer load must not be less than 5,000 VA or the nameplate rating if greater than 5 kW (for standard calculation); this does not apply to optional calculations. [220.54]

61. (b) 2/0 AWG, [Table 310.15(B)(6)]

62. (c) 70, [220.61(B)]

63. (c) 3/0 AWG

Table 310.15(B)(6) can be used only for the service/feeder conductors to individual dwelling units. For the service/feeder conductors that feed more than one individual dwelling unit, Table 310.15(B)(16) must be used to size conductors. [310.15(B)(6)]

64. (a) 110A, [220.82(B)]

General Loads

Step 1: Small-appliance and laundry circuits

Small-Appliance Circuits

1,500 VA x 2	3,000 VA
Laundry Circuit 1,500 VA	1,500 VA

Step 2: General Lighting

1,800 sq ft x 3 VA	5,400 VA

Step 3: Appliances (nameplate rating)

Water heater	4,000 VA
Dishwasher	1,500 VA
Dryer	4,500 VA
Ovens 3,000 VA x 2	6,000 VA
Range	6,000 VA

Step 4: Totals   31,900 VA

Step 5: Demand Factors

Total Connected Load= 31,900 VA

First 10,000 VA at 100%

10,000 VA at 100% =	10,000 VA

Remainder at 40%

21,900 VA at 40% =	8,760 VA

Step 6: Larger of A/C vs. Heat [220.82(C)]

A/C 100%: 6,000 VA	+ 6,000 VA

Heat 40%: 10,000W x 0.40 =

4,000 VA (Omit)

[220.82(C)(6)]

Step 7: Total Demand Load in VA

(Step 5 + Step 6)   24,760 VA

Step 8: Total Demand Load in Amperes:

I = P/E

I = 24,760 VA/240V

I = 103A would require at least 110A service

Step 9: Conductor size, 110A x 0.83 = 91.3A, 3 AWG
rated 100A, Table 310.15(B)(16)

65. (a) 48A

2 hp 115V motor FLC = 24A [Table 430.248]

Motor VA = V x A

Motor VA = 115V x 24A

Motor VA = 2,760 VA

L1	L2
1,900 VA	2,760 VA
1,900 VA	2,760 VA
1,900 VA	
5,700 VA	5,520 VA

Line 1 = 5,700 VA/120V = 47.50A

Line 2 = 5,520 VA/120V = 46A

Notes

Mike Holt's Journeyman Simulated Exam, based on the 2014 NEC

Take Your Training to the next level

& Save 25%

use discount code: B14JX25

2014 Master & Journeyman Comprehensive Exam Preparation Library

A complete course designed for your success. In-depth instruction for Theory and Code, with step-by-step instructions for solving electrical calculations. The DVDs are a vital component to learning, and the Practice Questions are key to reinforcing what you learn.

Understanding the National Electrical Code® Volumes 1 & 2 textbooks
Electrical Exam Preparation textbook
Basic Electrical Theory textbook
Simulated Exam
Code Review (10 DVDs)
Theory Review (3 DVDs)
Calculations Review (Masters - 8 DVDs; Journeyman - 5 DVDs)

Product Code: 14MACODVD	List Price: $1025.00	Now only $768.75
Product Code: 14JRCODVD	List Price: $925.00	Now only $693.75

2014 Masters Calculations DVD Library

Electrical Calculations apply to everybody. This is an ideal program whether you're preparing for an exam, or already working in the field. This program will teach you step by step how to properly set-up and solve electrical calculations.

Electrical Exam Preparation textbook
Raceway and Box Calculations DVD
Conductor Sizing and Protection Calculations DVD
Voltage-Drop Calculations DVD
Motor and Air-Conditioning Calculations DVD
Dwelling Unit Calculations DVD
Multifamily Dwelling Calculations DVD
Commercial Calculations DVD
Transformer Calculations DVD

Product Code: 14CADM   List Price: $599.00   Now only $449.25

2014 Detailed Code Library

There isn't a better way to learn the Code than Mike's Detailed Code Library.
Understanding the National Electrical Code® Volume 1 textbook
Understanding the National Electrical Code® Volume 2 textbook
NEC® Exam Practice Questions workbook
General Requirements DVD
Wiring and Protection DVD
Grounding vs. Bonding (2 DVDs)
Wiring Methods and Materials (2 DVDs)
Equipment for General Use DVD
Special Occupancies DVD
Special Equipment DVD
Limited Energy and Communications Systems DVD

Product Code: 14DECODVD   List Price: $569.00   Now only $426.75

Call Now 888.NEC.CODE (632.2633)

Mike Holt Enterprises, Inc.

All prices and availability are subject to change

PART 1

ELECTRICAL THEORY ANSWER SHEET

1. (a)(b)(c)(d)
2. (a)(b)(c)(d)
3. (a)(b)(c)(d)
4. (a)(b)(c)(d)
5. (a)(b)(c)(d)
6. (a)(b)(c)(d)
7. (a)(b)(c)(d)
8. (a)(b)(c)(d)
9. (a)(b)(c)(d)
10. (a)(b)(c)(d)
11. (a)(b)(c)(d)
12. (a)(b)(c)(d)
13. (a)(b)(c)(d)
14. (a)(b)(c)(d)
15. (a)(b)(c)(d)
16. (a)(b)(c)(d)
17. (a)(b)(c)(d)
18. (a)(b)(c)(d)
19. (a)(b)(c)(d)
20. (a)(b)(c)(d)
21. (a)(b)(c)(d)
22. (a)(b)(c)(d)
23. (a)(b)(c)(d)
24. (a)(b)(c)(d)
25. (a)(b)(c)(d)

26. (a)(b)(c)(d)
27. (a)(b)(c)(d)
28. (a)(b)(c)(d)
29. (a)(b)(c)(d)
30. (a)(b)(c)(d)
31. (a)(b)(c)(d)
32. (a)(b)(c)(d)
33. (a)(b)(c)(d)
34. (a)(b)(c)(d)
35. (a)(b)(c)(d)
36. (a)(b)(c)(d)
37. (a)(b)(c)(d)
38. (a)(b)(c)(d)
39. (a)(b)(c)(d)
40. (a)(b)(c)(d)
41. (a)(b)(c)(d)
42. (a)(b)(c)(d)
43. (a)(b)(c)(d)
44. (a)(b)(c)(d)
45. (a)(b)(c)(d)
46. (a)(b)(c)(d)
47. (a)(b)(c)(d)
48. (a)(b)(c)(d)
49. (a)(b)(c)(d)
50. (a)(b)(c)(d)

51. (a)(b)(c)(d)
52. (a)(b)(c)(d)
53. (a)(b)(c)(d)
54. (a)(b)(c)(d)
55. (a)(b)(c)(d)
56. (a)(b)(c)(d)
57. (a)(b)(c)(d)
58. (a)(b)(c)(d)
59. (a)(b)(c)(d)
60. (a)(b)(c)(d)
61. (a)(b)(c)(d)
62. (a)(b)(c)(d)
63. (a)(b)(c)(d)
64. (a)(b)(c)(d)
65. (a)(b)(c)(d)
66. (a)(b)(c)(d)
67. (a)(b)(c)(d)
68. (a)(b)(c)(d)
69. (a)(b)(c)(d)
70. (a)(b)(c)(d)
71. (a)(b)(c)(d)
72. (a)(b)(c)(d)
73. (a)(b)(c)(d)
74. (a)(b)(c)(d)
75. (a)(b)(c)(d)

76. (a)(b)(c)(d)
77. (a)(b)(c)(d)
78. (a)(b)(c)(d)
79. (a)(b)(c)(d)
80. (a)(b)(c)(d)
81. (a)(b)(c)(d)
82. (a)(b)(c)(d)
83. (a)(b)(c)(d)
84. (a)(b)(c)(d)
85. (a)(b)(c)(d)
86. (a)(b)(c)(d)
87. (a)(b)(c)(d)
88. (a)(b)(c)(d)
89. (a)(b)(c)(d)
90. (a)(b)(c)(d)
91. (a)(b)(c)(d)
92. (a)(b)(c)(d)
93. (a)(b)(c)(d)
94. (a)(b)(c)(d)
95. (a)(b)(c)(d)
96. (a)(b)(c)(d)
97. (a)(b)(c)(d)
98. (a)(b)(c)(d)
99. (a)(b)(c)(d)
100. (a)(b)(c)(d)

PART 2

NATIONAL ELECTRICAL CODE ANSWER SHEET

1. ⓐ ⓑ ⓒ ⓓ
2. ⓐ ⓑ ⓒ ⓓ
3. ⓐ ⓑ ⓒ ⓓ
4. ⓐ ⓑ ⓒ ⓓ
5. ⓐ ⓑ ⓒ ⓓ
6. ⓐ ⓑ ⓒ ⓓ
7. ⓐ ⓑ ⓒ ⓓ
8. ⓐ ⓑ ⓒ ⓓ
9. ⓐ ⓑ ⓒ ⓓ
10. ⓐ ⓑ ⓒ ⓓ
11. ⓐ ⓑ ⓒ ⓓ
12. ⓐ ⓑ ⓒ ⓓ
13. ⓐ ⓑ ⓒ ⓓ
14. ⓐ ⓑ ⓒ ⓓ
15. ⓐ ⓑ ⓒ ⓓ
16. ⓐ ⓑ ⓒ ⓓ
17. ⓐ ⓑ ⓒ ⓓ
18. ⓐ ⓑ ⓒ ⓓ
19. ⓐ ⓑ ⓒ ⓓ
20. ⓐ ⓑ ⓒ ⓓ
21. ⓐ ⓑ ⓒ ⓓ
22. ⓐ ⓑ ⓒ ⓓ
23. ⓐ ⓑ ⓒ ⓓ
24. ⓐ ⓑ ⓒ ⓓ
25. ⓐ ⓑ ⓒ ⓓ

26. ⓐ ⓑ ⓒ ⓓ
27. ⓐ ⓑ ⓒ ⓓ
28. ⓐ ⓑ ⓒ ⓓ
29. ⓐ ⓑ ⓒ ⓓ
30. ⓐ ⓑ ⓒ ⓓ
31. ⓐ ⓑ ⓒ ⓓ
32. ⓐ ⓑ ⓒ ⓓ
33. ⓐ ⓑ ⓒ ⓓ
34. ⓐ ⓑ ⓒ ⓓ
35. ⓐ ⓑ ⓒ ⓓ
36. ⓐ ⓑ ⓒ ⓓ
37. ⓐ ⓑ ⓒ ⓓ
38. ⓐ ⓑ ⓒ ⓓ
39. ⓐ ⓑ ⓒ ⓓ
40. ⓐ ⓑ ⓒ ⓓ
41. ⓐ ⓑ ⓒ ⓓ
42. ⓐ ⓑ ⓒ ⓓ
43. ⓐ ⓑ ⓒ ⓓ
44. ⓐ ⓑ ⓒ ⓓ
45. ⓐ ⓑ ⓒ ⓓ
46. ⓐ ⓑ ⓒ ⓓ
47. ⓐ ⓑ ⓒ ⓓ
48. ⓐ ⓑ ⓒ ⓓ
49. ⓐ ⓑ ⓒ ⓓ
50. ⓐ ⓑ ⓒ ⓓ

51. ⓐ ⓑ ⓒ ⓓ
52. ⓐ ⓑ ⓒ ⓓ
53. ⓐ ⓑ ⓒ ⓓ
54. ⓐ ⓑ ⓒ ⓓ
55. ⓐ ⓑ ⓒ ⓓ
56. ⓐ ⓑ ⓒ ⓓ
57. ⓐ ⓑ ⓒ ⓓ
58. ⓐ ⓑ ⓒ ⓓ
59. ⓐ ⓑ ⓒ ⓓ
60. ⓐ ⓑ ⓒ ⓓ
61. ⓐ ⓑ ⓒ ⓓ
62. ⓐ ⓑ ⓒ ⓓ
63. ⓐ ⓑ ⓒ ⓓ
64. ⓐ ⓑ ⓒ ⓓ
65. ⓐ ⓑ ⓒ ⓓ
66. ⓐ ⓑ ⓒ ⓓ
67. ⓐ ⓑ ⓒ ⓓ
68. ⓐ ⓑ ⓒ ⓓ
69. ⓐ ⓑ ⓒ ⓓ
70. ⓐ ⓑ ⓒ ⓓ
71. ⓐ ⓑ ⓒ ⓓ
72. ⓐ ⓑ ⓒ ⓓ
73. ⓐ ⓑ ⓒ ⓓ
74. ⓐ ⓑ ⓒ ⓓ
75. ⓐ ⓑ ⓒ ⓓ

76. ⓐ ⓑ ⓒ ⓓ
77. ⓐ ⓑ ⓒ ⓓ
78. ⓐ ⓑ ⓒ ⓓ
79. ⓐ ⓑ ⓒ ⓓ
80. ⓐ ⓑ ⓒ ⓓ
81. ⓐ ⓑ ⓒ ⓓ
82. ⓐ ⓑ ⓒ ⓓ
83. ⓐ ⓑ ⓒ ⓓ
84. ⓐ ⓑ ⓒ ⓓ
85. ⓐ ⓑ ⓒ ⓓ
86. ⓐ ⓑ ⓒ ⓓ
87. ⓐ ⓑ ⓒ ⓓ
88. ⓐ ⓑ ⓒ ⓓ
89. ⓐ ⓑ ⓒ ⓓ
90. ⓐ ⓑ ⓒ ⓓ
91. ⓐ ⓑ ⓒ ⓓ
92. ⓐ ⓑ ⓒ ⓓ
93. ⓐ ⓑ ⓒ ⓓ
94. ⓐ ⓑ ⓒ ⓓ
95. ⓐ ⓑ ⓒ ⓓ
96. ⓐ ⓑ ⓒ ⓓ
97. ⓐ ⓑ ⓒ ⓓ
98. ⓐ ⓑ ⓒ ⓓ
99. ⓐ ⓑ ⓒ ⓓ
100. ⓐ ⓑ ⓒ ⓓ

1. ⓐ ⓑ ⓒ ⓓ
2. ⓐ ⓑ ⓒ ⓓ
3. ⓐ ⓑ ⓒ ⓓ
4. ⓐ ⓑ ⓒ ⓓ
5. ⓐ ⓑ ⓒ ⓓ
6. ⓐ ⓑ ⓒ ⓓ
7. ⓐ ⓑ ⓒ ⓓ
8. ⓐ ⓑ ⓒ ⓓ
9. ⓐ ⓑ ⓒ ⓓ
10. ⓐ ⓑ ⓒ ⓓ
11. ⓐ ⓑ ⓒ ⓓ
12. ⓐ ⓑ ⓒ ⓓ
13. ⓐ ⓑ ⓒ ⓓ
14. ⓐ ⓑ ⓒ ⓓ
15. ⓐ ⓑ ⓒ ⓓ
16. ⓐ ⓑ ⓒ ⓓ

17. ⓐ ⓑ ⓒ ⓓ
18. ⓐ ⓑ ⓒ ⓓ
19. ⓐ ⓑ ⓒ ⓓ
20. ⓐ ⓑ ⓒ ⓓ
21. ⓐ ⓑ ⓒ ⓓ
22. ⓐ ⓑ ⓒ ⓓ
23. ⓐ ⓑ ⓒ ⓓ
24. ⓐ ⓑ ⓒ ⓓ
25. ⓐ ⓑ ⓒ ⓓ
26. ⓐ ⓑ ⓒ ⓓ
27. ⓐ ⓑ ⓒ ⓓ
28. ⓐ ⓑ ⓒ ⓓ
29. ⓐ ⓑ ⓒ ⓓ
30. ⓐ ⓑ ⓒ ⓓ
31. ⓐ ⓑ ⓒ ⓓ
32. ⓐ ⓑ ⓒ ⓓ

33. ⓐ ⓑ ⓒ ⓓ
34. ⓐ ⓑ ⓒ ⓓ
35. ⓐ ⓑ ⓒ ⓓ
36. ⓐ ⓑ ⓒ ⓓ
37. ⓐ ⓑ ⓒ ⓓ
38. ⓐ ⓑ ⓒ ⓓ
39. ⓐ ⓑ ⓒ ⓓ
40. ⓐ ⓑ ⓒ ⓓ
41. ⓐ ⓑ ⓒ ⓓ
42. ⓐ ⓑ ⓒ ⓓ
43. ⓐ ⓑ ⓒ ⓓ
44. ⓐ ⓑ ⓒ ⓓ
45. ⓐ ⓑ ⓒ ⓓ
46. ⓐ ⓑ ⓒ ⓓ
47. ⓐ ⓑ ⓒ ⓓ
48. ⓐ ⓑ ⓒ ⓓ

49. ⓐ ⓑ ⓒ ⓓ
50. ⓐ ⓑ ⓒ ⓓ
51. ⓐ ⓑ ⓒ ⓓ
52. ⓐ ⓑ ⓒ ⓓ
53. ⓐ ⓑ ⓒ ⓓ
54. ⓐ ⓑ ⓒ ⓓ
55. ⓐ ⓑ ⓒ ⓓ
56. ⓐ ⓑ ⓒ ⓓ
57. ⓐ ⓑ ⓒ ⓓ
58. ⓐ ⓑ ⓒ ⓓ
59. ⓐ ⓑ ⓒ ⓓ
60. ⓐ ⓑ ⓒ ⓓ
61. ⓐ ⓑ ⓒ ⓓ
62. ⓐ ⓑ ⓒ ⓓ
63. ⓐ ⓑ ⓒ ⓓ
64. ⓐ ⓑ ⓒ ⓓ
65. ⓐ ⓑ ⓒ ⓓ